THE ESSENTIAL WATER BATH CANNING & PRESERVING COOKBOOK FOR BEGINNERS

Step-by-Step Instructions for Safe, Long-Lasting Preserves, Traditional and Healthy Recipes for Every Season [FULL COLOR IMAGES]

By

ASHLEY COULTER

TABLE OF CONTENTS

CHAPTER 1

INTRODUCTION TO WATER BATH CANNING

1.1 THE BENEFITS OF CANNING

Water Bath Canning is a **traditional** and **safe** method for preserving low-acid foods. Using this technique, food is sealed in jars and immersedin boiling water for a set amount of time, sterilizing the contents and ensuring long-term preservation. Understanding the **benefits** of this practice will not only help you save money but also allow you to preserve the best flavors of the seasons in a natural way.

1.1.1 PRESERVING FLAVORS AND REDUCING WASTE

One of the biggest **advantages** of canning is the ability to **preserve the fresh, intense flavors** of seasonal ingredients all year round. There's nothing like opening a jar of strawberry jam in the middle of winter or using homemade tomato sauce to enhance your dishes. Every sealed jar becomes a memory of summer or harvest, offering an **authentic** and **genuine** culinary experience.

In addition, canning **dramatically reduces food waste**. How many times have you bought excess fruits or vegetables only for them to spoil? Preserving these foods allows you to maximize every resource, turning fresh produce into long-lasting preserves like **Classic Tomato Sauce**or delicious **Strawberry Jam**. Each jar represents both a financial saving and a commitment to **sustainability**.

1.1.2 SAVING MONEY AND FOOD SELF- SUFFICIENCY

Another important benefit of **water bath canning** is **cost savings**. Buying fruits and vegetables in season at lower prices and preserving them enables you to save significantly compared to purchasing commercially processed goods. Furthermore, preserving foods such as sauces, pickled vegetables, or homemade condiments helps you avoid the **additives** and **preservatives** found in store-bought products.

Canning also promotes **self-sufficiency**. Knowing you have a pantry stocked with foods you've prepared yourself provides a sense of satisfaction and security. Preparing preserves like **Classic Tomato Sauce** or **Pickled Vegetables** means you always have high-quality ingredients on hand, ready to use.

1.2 ESSENTIAL TOOLS AND EQUIPMENT

To successfully and safely preserve your food, it's important to have the right **tools**. The good news is that water bath canning requires onlya few basic tools, many of which you might already have in your kitchen. However, investing in **high-quality equipment** will ensure betterresults and ease of use.

1.2.1 OVERVIEW OF BASIC TOOLS

The essential tools for water bath canning include a large pot for the **water bath**, glass jars with lids and bands, jar lifters for handling the hot jars, and a funnel for filling them with the hot contents. Here's an overview of the most important items:

- ♦ **Water Bath Pot:** The pot must be large enough to hold the jars upright with at least 2-3 inches of water covering them. A rack atthe bottom of the pot prevents jars from touching the bottom and breaking.

- **Glass Jars:** Canning-specific glass jars are designed to withstand high temperatures and can be reused repeatedly. They come in different sizes (pint, quart, etc.) and should be chosen based on the quantity of product you want to preserve.
- **Lids and Bands:** Lids should be new for each use to guarantee an airtight seal, while bands can be reused as long as they aren'tdamaged or bent.
- **Jar Lifters:** This tool is essential for handling the hot jars, allowing you to remove them from the boiling water without riskingburns.
- **Funnel and Air Bubble Remover:** The funnel helps pour the hot food into the jars without spilling onto the rims, and the airbubble remover ensures that the contents of the jar are evenly distributed.

1.2.2 HOW TO CHOOSE JARS, LIDS, AND ACCESSORIES

Choosing the right jars is crucial for successful canning. There are jars of various sizes, but it's important to use those designed specifically for preservation, like the classic **Ball** or **Mason Jars**, which are built to withstand high temperatures. The most common sizes are **pint** and **quart**, and the choice will depend on the amount of food you intend to preserve.

Lids must be new each time to ensure a secure seal, while bands can be reused. It's important to choose high-quality lids and bands to avoidthem warping during the process.

CHAPTER 2
SAFETY IN CANNING

2.1 FUNDAMENTAL SAFETY PRINCIPLES

Safety is the most important element in home canning, and following a few fundamental rules is essential to ensure that your preserves are **safe to consume**. The water bath canning process is primarily used for **high-acid foods**, but properly managing acidity levels and sterilizationis critical to avoiding potential risks, such as **botulism**.

2.1.1 PREVENTING BOTULISM AND CONTAMINATIONS

Botulism is a serious illness caused by toxins produced by the *Clostridium botulinum* bacterium, which can grow in **oxygen-free environments**, like those created in sealed jars. The best way to prevent botulism is to ensure that preserved food is **sufficiently acidic** or processed correctly in the water bath.

The acidity level of foods is one of the key factors in preventing the growth of *Clostridium botulinum*. Acidic foods like tomatoes and fruits can be safely preserved using the water bath canning method as long as their **pH is below 4.6**. If a food has a higher pH, such as some vegetables, meats, or sauces, you will need to add **acid** (like lemon juice or vinegar) to lower the pH to a safe level.

In addition to acidity, it is crucial to properly **sterilize** jars, lids, and utensils to avoid harmful microorganisms contaminating the food. Contaminations can lead not only to botulism but also to other bacteria or molds that can spoil the product and pose a health risk.

2.1.2 MANAGING ACIDITY AND PH IN FOODS

Controlling **pH** is essential to ensuring safety in home canning. Foods such as fruits, jams, and tomato preserves are naturally acidic, but other ingredients, such as vegetables or legumes, require the addition of acid to be safe.

A practical example is the **acidification** of tomato sauce, as in the recipe for **Classic Tomato Sauce**: in this case, adding **lemon juice** or
vinegar not only enhances the flavor but also lowers the pH of the sauce, allowing it to be safely preserved using the water bath method.

To ensure the acidity level is correct, you can use tools like **pH test strips** or a **pH meter**, to verify that the value is below 4.6. This is especially important when preparing low-acid foods or when adding ingredients like herbs or spices that may alter the pH level.

2.2 PREPARATION AND STERILIZATION

Proper preparation of jars and equipment is a fundamental step to preventing contamination and ensuring that the preserved food is safe to consume long term. Each phase of the process, from sterilization to filling the jars, requires attention and care.

2.2.1 STERILIZING JARS AND EQUIPMENT

Before starting the canning process, it is essential to **sterilize** jars, lids, and all the equipment used. Even the slightest residue of bacteria can compromise the safety of the food. To sterilize the jars, fill a large pot with enough water to cover them and boil for at least **10 minutes**. Lidsand bands should also be sterilized but should not be boiled for more than 5 minutes to avoid deforming or damaging the sealing mechanism.

During sterilization, ensure the water completely covers the jars and lids. Once sterilized, keep the jars **hot** until you are ready to fill them, to prevent them from breaking when filled with hot food.

2.2.2 SAFELY FILLING JARS AND REMOVING AIR BUBBLES

Filling the jars must be done carefully to avoid contamination and ensure an airtight seal. First, pour the contents (whether sauce, jam, or pickled vegetables) into the jars using a **funnel**, leaving the recommended headspace as specified in the recipe. The space between the contents and the jar's rim, called the **headspace**, is important for creating the vacuum necessary to preserve the food.

Once the jars are filled, it is essential to **remove any air bubbles** trapped inside, using a non-metallic utensil to gently stir along the sides of the jar. Air bubbles can compromise the sealing process, leading to preservation failure or contamination.

Finally, carefully wipe the rims of the jars with a clean, damp cloth to remove any food or liquid residue that could interfere with sealing. Proper cleaning ensures that the lid can adhere perfectly to the jar, guaranteeing a long-term, safe seal.

CHAPTER 3

STEP-BY-STEP PROCESS

Following each phase carefully ensures that your food is safely preserved and the results are always optimal. From preparing the ingredients to properly processing the jars, paying attention to every detail is essential to ensure the best quality and safetyof your preserves.

3.1 PREPARING INGREDIENTS AND JARS

The first step to successful canning is the careful preparation of both the **ingredients** and the **jars**. Proper preparation not only enhances the quality of the preserved food but also helps prevent potential safety or quality issues during the canning process.

3.1.1 CLEANING, CUTTING, AND PREPARING THE FOOD

Thorough **cleaning** of the ingredients is essential to prevent contamination. Before beginning the process, it's important to wash fruits and vegetables under cold running water to remove dirt, pesticides, or other contaminants. Foods like tomatoes, for example, should be peeled before being preserved, while fruits like peaches may need to be sliced evenly to ensure uniform cooking.

Once cleaned, the ingredients should be **cut** into appropriately sized pieces. For preserves like **Classic Tomato Sauce**, tomatoes should be chopped into uniform pieces to ensure even cooking and the desired texture. Preparation also involves removing seeds, peels, or other unwanted parts that could affect the final result.

3.1.2 PREPARING AND FILLING THE JARS

After preparing the ingredients, the next step is to **prepare the jars**. As mentioned in previous chapters, the jars must be **properly sterilized** to avoid contamination. Once sterilized and kept warm, the jars are ready to be filled with the prepared food.

Filling the jars requires precision. Use a **funnel** to pour the food into the jars, leaving the recommended amount of **headspace** specified in the recipe. This space is important to allow the proper formation of a vacuum during the sealing process. For example, in **Classic Tomato Sauce**, it is recommended to leave about half an inch of space between the food and the rim of the jar.

After filling the jars, it's crucial to **remove any air bubbles** trapped inside. Use a non-metallic utensil to gently stir inside thejars, releasing any bubbles that could compromise the preservation process. After removing the bubbles, clean the rim of the jar with a damp cloth to ensure a perfect seal.

3.2 CANNING IN ACTION

Once the ingredients are prepared and the jars are filled, it's time to move on to the actual **canning process**. Proper placement of the jars in the canner and respecting the processing times and temperatures are key to ensuring the safety and quality of thefinal product.

3.2.1 CORRECT PLACEMENT OF JARS IN THE CANNER

After filling and sealing the jars, they must be correctly placed in the **canner**. First, ensure the canner is filled with enough hot water to completely cover the jars, with at least 2-3 inches of water above them. Use a **rack** at the bottom of the canner to prevent the jars from touching the bottom of the pot, which could cause them to break due to direct heat.

The jars must be placed **upright** and should not touch each other to avoid breaking during the boiling process. Ensure that thewater in the canner continues to boil gently throughout the process.

3.2.2 PROCESSING TIMES AND TEMPERATURES

The processing time is determined by the type of food being preserved and its acidity. Foods like fruits, jams, or tomato-based sauces require different boiling times than vegetables or meats. For example, **Classic Tomato Sauce** requires **40 minutes** of processing in a boiling water bath.

It is crucial to follow the recommended **times** and **temperatures** in the recipe to ensure that the food is properly preserved and safe to consume. If you live at a high altitude, you will need to **adjust the processing times** accordingly, as atmospheric pressure affects the boiling point of water.

Once the processing is complete, turn off the heat and let the jars rest in the water for a few minutes before removing them with jar lifters. Place them on a clean towel or rack to cool for at least **12-24 hours**, checking afterward that the lids are properly sealed.

For safe canning, it's essential to consider **altitude**. As altitude increases, **atmospheric pressure decreases**, which **lowers the boiling point of water**. This means that foods processed at higher altitudes require **longer boiling times** to reach the temperatures needed for safe preservation.

To adjust, add **1 additional minute of processing time** for every **1,000 feet** (about 300 meters) above sea level if you're canning at altitudes over **1,000 feet**. Check local altitude information if you're uncertain, as following these adjustments ensures **proper sterilization** and **safe storage** for all your preserved foods.

FUNDAMENTAL AND TRADITIONAL RECIPES

JAMS AND JELLIES

TRADITIONAL STRAWBERRY JAM

INGREDIENTS:

- 3 lbs of strawberries (about 1.36 kg), hulled and halved
- 4 cups of sugar (about 800 grams)
- 1/4 cup of lemon juice (about 60 ml)

INSTRUCTIONS:

1. **Prepare strawberries:** Mix strawberries and sugar in a large bowl. Let sit for 2-3 hours, stirring occasionally, until sugar dissolves and juices are released.
2. **Sterilize jars:** While waiting, sterilize jars and lids by boiling for 10 minutes. Keep hot until ready to use.
3. **Cook jam:** Transfer strawberry mixture to a large pot. Add lemon juice. Bring to a boil over medium-high heat, stirring frequently. Once boiling, reduce heat and simmer for 20-25 minutes until jam thickens. Skim off foam.
4. **Test consistency:** Place a spoonful of jam on a chilled plate. If it wrinkles when pushed, it's ready.
5. **Fill jars:** Ladle hot jam into jars, leaving 1/4 inch (6 mm) headspace. Remove air bubbles by tapping jars or using a non-metallic tool.
6. **Seal and process:** Wipe rims clean, place lids, and screw bands fingertip tight. Process in boiling water bath for 10 minutes, adjusting time for altitude.
7. **Cool and store:** Let jars cool for 12-24 hours. Check seals by pressing the lid center. Store sealed jars in a cool, dark place. Refrigerate any unsealed jars and use within a few weeks.

ADDITIONAL TIPS:

- For a chunkier jam, mash the strawberries to your desired consistency before cooking.
- You can substitute 1 cup of sugar with honey for a different flavor profile, but keep in mind it may slightly alter the texture.

TESTING AND CHECKING THE RECIPE:

- Remember the plate test for checking jam consistency. Having a few plates in the freezer before you start cooking will make this step easier.

STORAGE:

- Store jars in a cool, dark place. Properly sealed, the jam should last up to 1 year. Once opened, refrigerate and use within a month.

APPLE CINNAMON JELLY

INGREDIENTS:

- ♦ 4 cups of apple juice (about 950 ml), preferably freshly pressed
- ♦ 1/2 cup of lemon juice (about 120 ml)
- ♦ 4 cups of sugar (about 800 grams)
- ♦ 2 cinnamon sticks
- ♦ 1 package of powdered pectin (about 1.75 ounces or 50 grams)

INSTRUCTIONS:

1. **Prepare jars:** Sterilize jars and lids by boiling for 10 minutes. Keep hot until ready to use.
2. **Combine juices:** In a large pot, combine apple juice, lemon juice, and cinnamon sticks. Stir in pectin until dissolved. Bring to a rolling boil over high heat, stirring constantly.
3. **Add sugar:** Once boiling, add sugar all at once. Return to a rolling boil and cook for 1 minute, stirring constantly.
4. **Remove from heat:** Take off heat, discard cinnamon sticks, and skim off foam with a spoon.
5. **Fill jars:** Ladle hot jelly into jars, leaving 1/4 inch (6 mm) headspace. Remove air bubbles by tapping jars or using a non-metallic tool.
6. **Seal jars:** Wipe rims clean, place lids, and screw bands fingertip tight.
7. **Process in water bath:** Boil jars in a water bath for 10 minutes, adjusting for altitude if necessary.
8. **Cool and store:** Cool jars for 12-24 hours. Check seals by pressing the lid center. Store sealed jars in a cool, dark place.

ADDITIONAL TIPS:

- ♦ For a spicier flavor, you can add a few whole cloves or a small piece of fresh ginger to the pot in step 2.
- ♦ If you prefer a smoother jelly, you can strain the apple juice through a fine mesh sieve or cheesecloth before using.

TESTING AND CHECKING THE RECIPE:

- ♦ To test the jelly's consistency before canning, place a small spoonful on a chilled plate. If it gels and wrinkles when you push it with your finger, it's ready.

STORAGE:

- ♦ Store jars in a cool, dark place. Properly sealed, the jelly should last up to 1 year. Once opened, refrigerate and use within a month.

PEACH VANILLA JAM

INGREDIENTS:

- ♦ 5 lbs of peaches (about 2.27 kg), peeled, pitted, and chopped
- ♦ 2 cups of sugar (about 400 grams)
- ♦ 1 vanilla bean, split and scraped, or 1 tablespoon of vanilla extract
- ♦ 1/4 cup of lemon juice (about 60 ml)

INSTRUCTIONS:

1. **Prepare peaches:** Mix chopped peaches, lemon juice, and vanilla bean (or extract) in a large bowl. Let sit for 30 minutes to release juices.
2. **Sterilize jars:** While peaches macerate, sterilize jars and lids by boiling for 10 minutes. Keep hot until ready to use.
3. **Cook peach mixture:** Transfer peaches to a large pot, add sugar, and stir. Bring to a boil over medium-high heat, stirring frequently. Reduce heat and simmer for 20-25 minutes until thickened. Remove vanilla bean pod if used.
4. **Test consistency:** Place a small spoonful of jam on a chilled plate. If it wrinkles when pushed, it's ready.
5. **Fill jars:** Ladle hot jam into jars, leaving 1/4 inch (6 mm) headspace. Remove air bubbles by tapping jars or using a non-metallic tool.
6. **Seal and process:** Wipe rims clean, place lids, and screw bands fingertip tight. Process jars in a boiling water bath for 10 minutes, adjusting for altitude if necessary.
7. **Cool and store:** Cool jars for 12-24 hours. Check seals by pressing the lid center. Store sealed jars in a cool, dark place.

ADDITIONAL TIPS:

- ♦ For a smoother jam, you can puree the peaches in a blender or food processor before cooking.
- ♦ If you prefer a sweeter jam, you can adjust the amount of sugar according to your taste. However, keep in mind that sugar also acts as a preservative.

TESTING AND CHECKING THE RECIPE:

- ♦ The plate test is a simple way to check the consistency of your jam. Having a few plates in the freezer before you start cooking will make this step easier.

STORAGE:

- ♦ Store jars in a cool, dark place. Properly sealed, the jam should last up to 1 year. Once opened, refrigerate and use within a month.

BLUEBERRY LEMON JAM

INGREDIENTS:

- ◆ 4 cups of fresh blueberries (about 2 pints or 1.1 kg)
- ◆ 2 cups of sugar (about 400 grams)
- ◆ 1/4 cup of lemon juice (about 60 ml)
- ◆ Zest of 1 lemon
- ◆ 1 package of powdered pectin (about 1.75 ounces or 50 grams)

INSTRUCTIONS:

1. **Prepare blueberries:** Wash and drain blueberries. Crush with a potato masher or pulse in a food processor for a smoother texture.
2. **Sterilize jars:** Sterilize jars and lids by boiling for 10 minutes. Keep hot until ready to use.
3. **Mix berries with lemon and pectin:** In a large pot, combine crushed blueberries, lemon juice, and zest. Sprinkle pectin and stir until blended.
4. **Bring to boil:** Bring mixture to a rolling boil over high heat, stirring constantly.
5. **Add sugar:** Stir in sugar all at once. Return to a rolling boil and boil hard for 1 minute, stirring constantly.
6. **Remove from heat and skim foam:** Take off heat and skim foam with a spoon.
7. **Fill jars:** Ladle hot jam into jars, leaving 1/4 inch (6 mm) headspace. Remove air bubbles by tapping jars or using a non-metallic tool.
8. **Seal and process:** Wipe rims clean, place lids, and screw bands fingertip tight. Process jars in a boiling water bath for 10 minutes, adjusting for altitude if necessary.
9. **Cool and store:** Cool jars for 12-24 hours. Check seals by pressing the lid center. Store sealed jars in a cool, dark place.

ADDITIONAL TIPS:

- ◆ For a less sweet jam, you can reduce the sugar by up to 1/2 cup. However, keep in mind that sugar helps with the preservation and setting of the jam.
- ◆ Adding a small knob of butter or margarine with the berries can help reduce foaming during boiling.

TESTING AND CHECKING THE RECIPE:

- ◆ To test the jam's consistency before canning, place a small spoonful on a chilled plate. If it gels and wrinkles when you push it with your finger, it's ready.

STORAGE:

- ◆ Store jars in a cool, dark place. Properly sealed, the jam should last up to 1 year. Once opened, refrigerate and use within a month.

NATURAL GRAPE JELLY

INGREDIENTS:

- 4 cups of grape juice (about 950 ml), preferably from Concordgrapes
- 1/2 cup of lemon juice (about 120 ml)
- 4 cups of sugar (about 800 grams)
- 1 package of powdered pectin (about 1.75 ounces or 50 grams)

INSTRUCTIONS:

1. **Prepare grape juice:** If using fresh grapes, wash, crush, and simmer for 10 minutes. Strain through a fine sieve or cheesecloth. Measure 4 cups of juice.
2. **Sterilize jars:** Sterilize jars and lids by boiling for 10 minutes. Keep hot until ready to use.
3. **Mix juice with lemon and pectin:** In a large pot, combine grape juice and lemon juice. Sprinkle pectin and stir until blended.
4. **Bring to boil:** Bring mixture to a rolling boil over high heat, stirring constantly.
5. **Add sugar:** Stir in sugar all at once. Return to a rolling boil and boil hard for 1 minute, stirring constantly.
6. **Remove from heat and skim foam:** Take off heat and skim foam with a spoon.
7. **Fill jars:** Ladle hot jelly into jars, leaving 1/4 inch (6 mm) headspace. Remove air bubbles by tapping jars or using a non-metallic tool.
8. **Seal and process:** Wipe rims clean, place lids, and screw bands fingertip tight. Process jars in a boiling water bath for 10 minutes, adjusting for altitude if necessary.
9. **Cool and store:** Cool jars for 12-24 hours. Check seals by pressing the lid center. Store sealed jars in a cool, dark place.

ADDITIONAL TIPS:

- For a clearer jelly, let the juice sit overnight in the refrigerator after straining to allow any remaining sediment to settle at the bottom. Carefully pour off the clear juice for use in your jelly.
- You can reduce the sugar by up to 1 cup if you prefer a less sweet jelly, but keep in mind that sugar helps with the preservation and setting of the jelly.

TESTING AND CHECKING THE RECIPE:

- To test the jelly's consistency before canning, place a small spoonful on a chilled plate. If it gels and wrinkles when you push it with your finger, it's ready.

STORAGE:

- Store jars in a cool, dark place. Properly sealed, the jelly should last up to 1 year. Once opened, refrigerate and use within a month.

APRICOT HONEY JAM

INGREDIENTS:

- ♦ 4 lbs of apricots (about 1.8 kg), halved and pitted
- ♦ 2 cups of honey (about 480 ml)
- ♦ 1/2 cup of lemon juice (about 120 ml)
- ♦ 1/4 cup of water (about 60 ml)

INSTRUCTIONS:

1. **Prepare apricots:** Toss apricot halves with lemon juice to prevent browning and add tanginess.
2. **Cook mixture:** In a large pot, combine apricots, honey, and water. Stir over medium heat until honey dissolves and mixture simmers.
3. **Simmer jam:** Reduce heat to low and cook for 25-30 minutes, stirring occasionally, until apricots soften and mixture thickens slightly.
4. **Mash apricots:** Mash apricots to desired consistency using a potato masher or spoon.
5. **Sterilize jars:** While cooking, sterilize jars and lids by boiling for 10 minutes. Keep hot until ready to use.
6. **Fill jars:** Ladle hot jam into jars, leaving 1/4 inch (6 mm) headspace. Remove air bubbles by tapping jars or using a non-metallic tool.
7. **Seal and process:** Wipe rims clean, place lids, and screw bands fingertip tight. Process in a boiling water bath for 10 minutes, adjusting for altitude if needed.
8. **Cool and store:** Cool jars for 12-24 hours. Check seals by pressing lid center. Store sealed jars in a cool, dark place.

ADDITIONAL TIPS:

- ♦ For a more robust flavor, you can add a teaspoon of vanilla extract or a cinnamon stick during the cooking process. Just remember to remove the cinnamon stick before canning.
- ♦ If the jam is too thick, you can add a little more water during the cooking process. If it's too thin, continue cooking it for a longer period to reduce and thicken.

TESTING AND CHECKING THE RECIPE:

- ♦ To test the jam's consistency before canning, place a small spoonful on a chilled plate. If it gels and wrinkles when you push it with your finger, it's ready.

STORAGE:

- ♦ Store jars in a cool, dark place. Properly sealed, the jam should last up to 1 year. Once opened, refrigerate and use within a month.

POMEGRANATE JELLY

INGREDIENTS:

- 4 cups pomegranate juice (about 950 ml), freshly squeezed for bestflavor
- 1/2 cup lemon juice (about 120 ml), freshly squeezed
- 5 cups sugar (about 1 kg)
- 1 package powdered pectin (about 1.75 ounces or 50 grams)

INSTRUCTIONS:

1. **Prepare jars:** Sterilize jars and lids by boiling for 10 minutes. Keep hot until ready to use.
2. **Mix juices:** In a large pot, combine pomegranate and lemon juice. Sprinkle pectin over the juice and let it sit for a few minutes to dissolve.
3. **Heat mixture:** Bring to a rolling boil over medium-high heat, stirring constantly to prevent sticking.
4. **Add sugar:** Stir in sugar all at once. Return to a rolling boil and boil hard for 1 minute, stirring constantly.
5. **Remove from heat and skim foam:** Take off heat and skim foam with a spoon for a clearer jelly.
6. **Fill jars:** Ladle hot jelly into jars, leaving 1/4 inch (6 mm) headspace. Remove air bubbles by tapping jars or using a non-metallic tool.
7. **Seal jars:** Wipe rims clean, place lids, and screw bands fingertip tight.
8. **Process in water bath:** Boil jars in a water bath for 10 minutes, adjusting for altitude if needed.
9. **Cool and store:** Cool jars for 12-24 hours. Check seals by pressing lid center. Store sealed jars in a cool, dark place.

ADDITIONAL TIPS:

- For an extra kick, add a cinnamon stick or a few cloves to the pot while cooking the jelly mixture. Just remember to remove them before canning.
- If you prefer a less sweet jelly, you can reduce the sugar by up to 1 cup, but keep in mind that sugar helps with the preservation and setting of the jelly.

TESTING AND CHECKING THE RECIPE:

- To test the jelly's consistency before canning, place a small spoonful on a chilled plate. If it gels and wrinkles when you push it with your finger, it's ready.

STORAGE:

- Store jars in a cool, dark place. Properly sealed, the jelly should last up to 1 year. Once opened, refrigerate and use within a month.

RASPBERRY GINGER JAM

- 4 cups of raspberries (about 0.9 kg)
- 2 cups of sugar (about 400 grams)
- 1/4 cup of lemon juice (about 60 ml)
- 2 tablespoons of freshly grated ginger (about 30 grams)

INSTRUCTIONS:

1. **Prepare raspberries:** Gently rinse raspberries and drain thoroughly.
2. **Macerate:** Combine raspberries and sugar in a bowl, letting them sit for 30 minutes to release juices.
3. **Sterilize jars:** While waiting, sterilize jars and lids by boiling for 10 minutes. Keep hot until ready to use.
4. **Cook mixture:** In a large pot, combine raspberry mixture, lemon juice, and grated ginger. Stir well.
5. **Bring to boil:** Over medium-high heat, bring to a rolling boil, stirring frequently.
6. **Boil until set:** Reduce heat slightly and boil for 15-20 minutes until thickened. Test readiness using the chilled plate method.
7. **Remove from heat:** Skim off any foam from the top with a spoon.
8. **Fill jars:** Ladle hot jam into jars, leaving 1/4 inch (6 mm) headspace. Remove air bubbles by tapping jars or using a non-metallic tool.
9. **Seal jars:** Wipe rims clean, place lids, and screw bands fingertip tight.
10. **Process in water bath:** Boil jars in a water bath for 10 minutes, adjusting for altitude if needed.
11. **Cool and store:** Cool jars for 12-24 hours. Check seals by pressing the lid center. Store sealed jars in a cool, dark place.

ADDITIONAL TIPS:

- For a spicier jam, you can add more ginger according to your taste. However, start with the recommended amount and adjust in future batches to avoid overpowering the raspberries.
- If you find the jam too sweet, you can slightly increase the amount of lemon juice to add more tartness, balancing the flavors.

TESTING AND CHECKING THE RECIPE:

- The plate test is a simple way to check the consistency of your jam. Having a few plates in the freezer before you start cooking will make this step easier.

STORAGE:

- Store jars in a cool, dark place. Properly sealed, the jam should last up to 1 year. Once opened, refrigerate and use within a month.

BITTER ORANGE JELLY

INGREDIENTS:

- ◆ 4 cups of bitter orange juice (about 950 ml)
- ◆ 1/2 cup of lemon juice (about 120 ml)
- ◆ 5 cups of sugar (about 1 kg)
- ◆ 1 package powdered pectin (about 1.75 ounces or 50 grams)

INSTRUCTIONS:

1. **Prepare jars:** Sterilize jars and lids by boiling for 10 minutes. Keep hot until ready to use.
2. **Mix juices:** In a large pot, combine bitter orange and lemon juice. Sprinkle pectin over the juice and let sit for a few minutes to dissolve.
3. **Heat mixture:** Bring to a rolling boil over medium-high heat, stirring constantly to prevent sticking.
4. **Add sugar:** Stir in sugar all at once. Return to a rolling boil and boil hard for 1 minute, stirring constantly.
5. **Remove from heat and skim foam:** Take off heat and skim foam with a spoon for a clearer jelly.
6. **Fill jars:** Ladle hot jelly into jars, leaving 1/4 inch (6 mm) headspace. Remove air bubbles by tapping jars or using a non-metallic tool.
7. **Seal jars:** Wipe rims clean, place lids, and screw bands fingertip tight.
8. **Process in water bath:** Boil jars in a water bath for 10 minutes, adjusting for altitude if necessary.
9. **Cool and store:** Cool jars for 12-24 hours. Check seals by pressing the lid center. Store sealed jars in a cool, dark place.

ADDITIONAL TIPS:

- ◆ For a less bitter taste, you can mix the bitter orange juice with sweet orange juice, but keep the total juice volume thesame.
- ◆ Adding a small piece of the orange peel to each jar before sealing can enhance the flavor, but ensure to remove any white pith to avoid bitterness.

TESTING AND CHECKING THE RECIPE:

- ◆ To test the jelly's consistency before canning, place a small spoonful on a chilled plate. If it gels and wrinkles when you push it with your finger, it's ready.

STORAGE:

- ◆ Store jars in a cool, dark place. Properly sealed, the jelly should last up to 1 year. Once opened, refrigerate and use within a month.

PEAR SAFFRON JAM

INGREDIENTS:

- 6 cups of peeled, cored, and chopped pears (about 3 lbs or 1.36 kg)
- 3 cups of sugar (about 600 grams)
- 1/2 cup of water (about 120 ml)
- Juice of 1 lemon (about 2 tablespoons or 30 ml)
- 1 teaspoon of saffron threads (about 0.1 gram)

INSTRUCTIONS:

1. **Prepare pears:** Peel, core, and chop pears into small pieces for even cooking.
2. **Combine pears with lemon and water:** In a large pot, mix pears with lemon juice and water to prevent browning.
3. **Add saffron:** Sprinkle saffron threads over the pear mixture for color and flavor.
4. **Cook mixture:** Cook over medium heat, stirring occasionally until pears soften. Increase heat to medium-high.
5. **Add sugar:** Once simmering, add sugar and stir until dissolved. Cook, stirring frequently to prevent sticking.
6. **Bring to a boil:** Increase heat to high and bring to a rolling boil that cannot be stirred down. Boil for 10-15 minutes until thickened.
7. **Test consistency:** Use the chilled plate method to check readiness—if it wrinkles when pushed, the jam is ready.
8. **Sterilize jars:** While cooking, sterilize jars and lids by boiling for 10 minutes.
9. **Fill jars:** Ladle hot jam into jars, leaving 1/4 inch (6 mm) headspace. Remove air bubbles.
10. **Seal jars:** Wipe rims clean, place lids, and screw bands fingertip tight.
11. **Process in water bath:** Boil jars in water for 10 minutes, adjusting for altitude if necessary.
12. **Cool and store:** Cool jars for 12-24 hours. Check seals and store in a cool, dark place.

ADDITIONAL TIPS:

- For a more intense saffron flavor, let the saffron threads steep in a tablespoon of hot water for about 10 minutes before adding it to the pears.
- If you prefer a smoother jam, you can use an immersion blender to puree the jam to your desired consistency before fillingthe jars.

TESTING AND CHECKING THE RECIPE:

- The plate test is a simple and effective way to check the consistency of your jam. Place a small spoonful of jam on a plate that has been chilled in the freezer; if it gels and wrinkles when pushed, it's ready.

STORAGE:

- Store jars in a cool, dark place. Properly sealed, the jam should last up to 1 year. Once opened, refrigerate and use within amonth.

CLASSIC TOMATO SAUCE

INGREDIENTS:

- 10 lbs of ripe tomatoes (about 4.5 kg), peeled and chopped
- 2 cups of chopped onions (about 300 grams)
- 1 cup of chopped bell peppers (about 150 grams)
- 5 cloves of garlic, minced
- 1/4 cup of olive oil (about 60 ml)
- 1/4 cup of fresh basil leaves, chopped (about 15 grams)
- 2 tablespoons of fresh oregano leaves, chopped (about 30 grams)
- 1 tablespoon of salt (about 15 grams)
- 1 teaspoon of ground black pepper (about 5 grams)
- 1/2 cup of lemon juice (about 120 ml), for acidification

INSTRUCTIONS:

1. **Prepare tomatoes:** Blanch tomatoes in boiling water for 30-60 seconds until skins peel. Transfer to an ice bath, peel, and chop.
2. **Cook vegetables:** In a large pot, heat olive oil over medium heat. Sauté onions, bell peppers, and garlic for 5-7 minutes until soft.
3. **Add tomatoes and herbs:** Stir in tomatoes, basil, oregano, salt, and black pepper. Bring to a simmer over medium heat.
4. **Simmer sauce:** Reduce heat to low and cook uncovered for about 2 hours until thickened, stirring occasionally.
5. **Acidify sauce:** Stir in lemon juice for safe water bath canning.
6. **Prepare jars:** While sauce cooks, sterilize jars and lids by boiling for 10 minutes. Keep hot until ready to use.
7. **Fill jars:** Ladle hot sauce into jars, leaving 1/2 inch (12 mm) headspace. Remove air bubbles.
8. **Seal jars:** Wipe rims clean, place lids, and screw bands fingertip tight.
9. **Process in water bath:** Boil jars in water bath for 40 minutes, adjusting for altitude if necessary.
10. **Cool and store**: Cool jars for 12-24 hours. Check seals by pressing the lid center. Store in a cool, dark place.

ADDITIONAL TIPS:

- For a smoother sauce, you can blend the cooked sauce with an immersion blender before canning.
- If you prefer a spicier sauce, add chopped chili peppers or red pepper flakes during the cooking process.

TESTING AND CHECKING THE RECIPE:

- To ensure safety, use a pH meter or test strips to check that the sauce's pH is below 4.6, which is safe for water bath canning.

STORAGE:

- Store jars in a cool, dark place. Properly sealed, the sauce should last up to 1 year. Once opened, refrigerate and use within a week

BASIL GREEN SAUCE

INGREDIENTS:

- ◆ 2 cups fresh basil leaves, packed (about 80 grams)
- ◆ 1/2 cup grated Parmesan cheese (about 45 grams)
- ◆ 1/2 cup extra virgin olive oil (about 120 ml)
- ◆ 1/3 cup pine nuts (about 45 grams)
- ◆ 3 garlic cloves, minced
- ◆ Salt and pepper to taste
- ◆ 2 tablespoons lemon juice (about 30 ml), for acidification

INSTRUCTIONS:

1. **Prepare basil:** Rinse basil leaves and pat dry with a paper towel.
2. **Toast pine nuts:** Toast pine nuts in a skillet over medium heat for 2-3 minutes until golden, stirring constantly.
3. **Combine ingredients:** In a food processor, combine basil, toasted pine nuts, garlic, and Parmesan. Pulse to chop and blend.
4. **Add olive oil:** With the processor running, slowly pour in olive oil to emulsify.
5. **Season sauce:** Add salt and pepper to taste, then pulse to mix. Adjust seasoning if necessary.
6. **Acidify sauce:** Stir in lemon juice by hand to ensure safe acidity for canning.
7. **Prepare jars:** Sterilize jars and lids by boiling for 10 minutes. Keep hot until ready to use.
8. **Fill jars:** Ladle salsa into jars, leaving 1/2 inch (12 mm) headspace. Remove air bubbles.
9. **Seal jars:** Wipe rims clean, place lids, and screw bands fingertip tight.
10. **Process in water bath:** Boil jars in water bath for 15 minutes, adjusting for altitude if needed.
11. **Cool and store**: Cool jars for 12-24 hours. Check seals by pressing lid center. Store in a cool, dark place.

ADDITIONAL TIPS:

- ◆ For a variation, try using walnuts or almonds instead of pine nuts for a different flavor profile.
- ◆ If you prefer a vegan version, you can omit the Parmesan cheese or use a nutritional yeast substitute.

TESTING AND CHECKING THE RECIPE:

- ◆ To ensure the salsa verde has the correct acidity for safe canning, use a pH meter or test strips to check that the sauce's pH is below 4.6.

STORAGE:

- ◆ Store jars in a cool, dark place. Properly sealed, the salsa should last up to 1 year. Once opened, refrigerate and use within a month.

RED ONION CHUTNEY

INGREDIENTS:

- 4 large red onions, thinly sliced (about 2 lbs or 0.9 kg)
- 1 cup (240 ml) apple cider vinegar
- 1/2 cup (100 grams) brown sugar
- 1/4 cup (50 grams) white sugar
- 1 teaspoon (5 grams) salt
- 1/2 teaspoon (2 grams) ground black pepper
- 1/2 teaspoon (1 gram) crushed red pepper flakes (optional for heat)
- 1 teaspoon (2 grams) mustard seeds
- 1/4 cup (60 ml) balsamic vinegar
- 1 cinnamon stick

INSTRUCTIONS:

1. **Prepare onions:** Peel and slice onions evenly.
2. **Combine vinegars, sugars, and spices:** In a large pot, mix apple cider vinegar, sugars, salt, black pepper, red pepper flakes (optional), mustard seeds, and cinnamon stick. Stir to dissolve.
3. **Heat mixture:** Simmer over medium heat, stirring occasionally to dissolve sugars.
4. **Add onions:** Add sliced onions and stir to coat with the vinegar mixture.
5. **Simmer chutney:** Reduce heat to low and simmer for 30-40 minutes, stirring occasionally, until onions are tender and liquid thickens.
6. **Prepare jars:** While chutney cooks, sterilize jars and lids by boiling for 10 minutes.
7. **Fill jars:** Ladle hot chutney into jars, leaving 1/2 inch (12 mm) headspace. Remove cinnamon stick. Remove air bubbles by tapping jars or using a non-metallic tool.
8. **Seal jars:** Wipe rims clean, place lids, and screw bands fingertip tight.
9. **Process in water bath:** Boil jars in a water bath for 10 minutes, adjusting for altitude if needed.
10. **Cool and store**: Cool jars for 12-24 hours. Check seals by pressing the lid center. Store in a cool, dark place.

ADDITIONAL TIPS:

- For a variation, try adding raisins or chopped apples to the chutney for a fruitier flavor.
- If you prefer a smoother chutney, you can use an immersion blender to lightly puree the mixture before filling the jars.

TESTING AND CHECKING THE RECIPE:

- To check the consistency of your chutney before canning, place a small spoonful on a chilled plate. If it thickens to your liking as it cools, it's ready.

STORAGE:

- Store jars in a cool, dark place. Properly sealed, the chutney should last up to 1 year. Once opened, refrigerate and use within a month.

SMOKY BARBECUE SAUCE

- 2 cups ketchup (about 480 ml)
- 1/2 cup apple cider vinegar (about 120 ml)
- 1/2 cup brown sugar, packed (about 100 grams)
- 1/4 cup honey (about 60 ml)
- 2 tablespoons Worcestershire sauce (about 30 ml)
- 2 tablespoons smoked paprika (about 30 grams)
- 1 tablespoon garlic powder (about 15 grams)
- 1 teaspoon ground mustard (about 5 grams)
- 1/2 teaspoon ground black pepper (about 2.5 grams)
- 1/2 teaspoon salt (about 2.5 grams)
- 1/4 teaspoon cayenne pepper (optional for heat) (about 1.25 grams)
- 1 cup water (about 240 ml)

INSTRUCTIONS:

1. **Combine ingredients:** In a large saucepan, mix ketchup, vinegar, brown sugar, honey, Worcestershire sauce, smoked paprika, garlic powder, ground mustard, black pepper, salt, cayenne (if using), and water.
2. **Cook sauce:** Heat the mixture over medium heat, stirring frequently until it simmers.
3. **Simmer:** Reduce heat to low and cook for 20-25 minutes, stirring occasionally until the sauce thickens.
4. **Taste and adjust:** Taste and adjust seasoning, adding more cayenne for heat if needed.
5. **Prepare jars:** While cooking, sterilize jars and lids by boiling for 10 minutes.
6. **Fill jars:** Ladle hot sauce into jars, leaving 1/2 inch (12 mm) headspace. Remove air bubbles.
7. **Seal jars:** Wipe rims clean, place lids, and screw bands fingertip tight.
8. **Process in water bath:** Boil jars in a water bath for 20 minutes, adjusting for altitude if needed.
9. **Cool and store:** Cool jars for 12-24 hours. Check seals by pressing the lid center. Store in a cool, dark place.

ADDITIONAL TIPS:

- For a smoother sauce, you can blend the mixture with an immersion blender before canning.
- If you prefer a sweeter sauce, adjust the amount of honey or brown sugar to taste.

TESTING AND CHECKING THE RECIPE:

- To ensure the sauce is at the right consistency before canning, you can place a small spoonful on a plate and refrigerate it for a few minutes. If it thickens to your liking, it's ready.

STORAGE:

- Store jars in a cool, dark place. Properly sealed, the sauce should last up to 1 year. Once opened, refrigerate and use within a month.

SPICY CHILI SAUCE

INGREDIENTS:

- 1 lb (450g) fresh chili peppers (mix of jalapeño, serrano, and habanero for varied heat)
- 3 cups (720ml) distilled white vinegar
- 2 cups (400g) granulated sugar
- 1 tablespoon (15g) salt
- 6 cloves garlic, minced
- 1 teaspoon (5g) cumin seeds
- 1/2 teaspoon (2.5g) black peppercorns

INSTRUCTIONS:

1. **Prepare chili peppers:** Wash and finely chop the peppers (wear gloves). Remove seeds and membranes for a milder sauce.
2. **Combine vinegar, sugar, and spices:** In a large pot, mix vinegar, sugar, salt, garlic, cumin seeds, and peppercorns. Stir over medium heat until sugar dissolves.
3. **Add chopped peppers:** Add chopped chili peppers to the pot and stir well.
4. **Bring to boil:** Increase heat to bring mixture to a boil, then reduce to a simmer.
5. **Simmer salsa:** Simmer for 10-15 minutes, stirring occasionally until slightly thickened.
6. **Prepare jars:** While salsa simmers, sterilize jars and lids by boiling for 10 minutes.
7. **Fill jars:** Ladle hot salsa into jars, leaving 1/2 inch (12 mm) headspace. Remove air bubbles.
8. **Seal jars:** Wipe rims clean, place lids, and screw bands fingertip tight.
9. **Process in water bath:** Boil jars in water bath for 15 minutes, adjusting for altitude if necessary.
10. **Cool and store:** Cool jars for 12-24 hours. Check seals by pressing the lid center. Store in a cool, dark place.

ADDITIONAL TIPS:

- For a smoother salsa, you can blend the mixture before canning.
- Adjust the mix of chili peppers based on your heat preference. More habanero peppers will increase the heat, while more jalapeños will make it milder.

TESTING AND CHECKING THE RECIPE:

- To test the salsa's flavor before canning, let it cool slightly and taste. Adjust the seasoning if necessary.

STORAGE:

- Store jars in a cool, dark place. Properly sealed, the salsa should last up to 1 year. Once opened, refrigerate and use within a month.

DILL PICKLES

INGREDIENTS:

- 4 lbs (about 1.8 kg) pickling cucumbers, washed and sliced into 1/4 inch (about 6 mm) rounds
- 4 cups (about 950 ml) water
- 4 cups (about 950 ml) white vinegar
- 1/3 cup (about 75 grams) pickling salt
- 2 tablespoons (about 30 grams) sugar
- 8 cloves garlic, peeled and halved
- 4 teaspoons (about 20 grams) dill seeds
- 8 fresh dill sprigs
- 4 teaspoons (about 20 grams) mustard seeds
- 2 teaspoons (about 10 grams) black peppercorns
- 4 clean pint-sized (about 473 ml) canning jars with lids and bands

INSTRUCTIONS:

1. **Prepare cucumbers:** Wash cucumbers and slice into 1/4 inch rounds.
2. **Sterilize jars:** Boil jars and lids for 10 minutes to sterilize. Keep hot until ready to use.
3. **Make brine:** In a large pot, combine water, vinegar, salt, and sugar. Bring to a boil, stirring until dissolved.
4. **Pack jars:** Place garlic, dill seeds, dill sprigs, mustard seeds, and peppercorns in each jar. Pack cucumbers tightly, leaving 1/2 inch (12 mm) headspace.
5. **Fill jars with brine:** Ladle hot brine over cucumbers, leaving 1/2 inch headspace. Remove air bubbles.
6. **Seal jars:** Wipe rims clean, place lids, and screw bands fingertip tight.
7. **Process in water bath:** Boil jars in a water bath for 10 minutes, adjusting for altitude if necessary.
8. **Cool and store:** Cool jars for 12-24 hours. Check seals by pressing the lid center. Store in a cool, dark place.

ADDITIONAL TIPS:

- For crisper pickles, add a grape leaf to each jar before adding the cucumbers.
- If you prefer a spicier kick, add a small chili pepper or a few red pepper flakes to each jar.

TESTING AND CHECKING THE RECIPE:

- To ensure the pickles have the right flavor and texture, let them sit in the sealed jars for at least 2 weeks before opening. This allows the flavors to develop fully.

STORAGE:

- Store jars in a cool, dark place. Properly sealed, the pickles should last up to 1 year. Once opened, refrigerate and consume within a month.

SWEET PICKLED PEPPERS

INGREDIENTS:

- 6 large sweet bell peppers (red, yellow, or orange), sliced into strips (about 3 lbs or 1.36 kg)
- 4 cups white vinegar (about 950 ml)
- 2 cups water (about 475 ml)
- 2 tablespoons pickling salt (about 30 grams)
- 2 tablespoons sugar (about 25 grams)
- 4 cloves garlic, peeled and halved
- 2 teaspoons black peppercorns (about 10 grams)
- 4 bay leaves

INSTRUCTIONS:

1. **Sterilize jars:** Boil jars and lids for 10 minutes to sterilize. Keep hot until ready to use.
2. **Prepare peppers:** Wash, stem, and seed peppers, then slice into 1/4 inch strips.
3. **Make brine:** In a large pot, combine vinegar, water, salt, and sugar. Bring to a boil, stirring until dissolved.
4. **Add peppers to brine:** Add sliced peppers to the boiling brine and cook for 2 minutes.
5. **Pack jars:** Place garlic, peppercorns, and a bay leaf in each jar. Pack peppers tightly into the jars.
6. **Fill jars with brine:** Ladle hot brine over peppers, leaving 1/2 inch (12 mm) headspace. Remove air bubbles.
7. **Seal jars:** Wipe rims clean, place lids, and screw bands fingertip tight.
8. **Process in water bath:** Boil jars in a water bath for 10 minutes, adjusting for altitude if necessary.
9. **Cool and store:** Cool jars for 12-24 hours. Check seals by pressing the lid center. Store in a cool, dark place.

ADDITIONAL TIPS:

- For a spicier variation, add a small chili pepper or a teaspoon of crushed red pepper flakes to each jar before adding the brine.
- If you prefer a sweeter pickled pepper, increase the sugar in the brine to 1/4 cup (about 50 grams).

TESTING AND CHECKING THE RECIPE:

- To ensure the peppers are properly pickled, check the jars after 24 hours to make sure the lids have sealed by pressing down in the center of each lid. If the lid pops back, it's not sealed and should be refrigerated and used first.

STORAGE:

- Store jars in a cool, dark place. Properly sealed, the pickled peppers should last up to 1 year. Once opened, refrigerate and use within a month.

SWEET AND SOUR WHITE ONIONS

- 3 lbs (about 1.36 kg) white onions, peeled and thinly sliced
- 2 cups (about 480 ml) apple cider vinegar
- 1 cup (about 200 grams) granulated sugar
- 1 tablespoon (about 15 grams) salt
- 1 teaspoon (about 2 grams) turmeric
- 1 teaspoon (about 2 grams) mustard seeds
- 1/2 teaspoon (about 1 gram) celery seeds
- 1/4 teaspoon (about 0.5 grams) ground cloves
- 2 cups (about 480 ml) water

INSTRUCTIONS:

1. **Prepare onions:** Peel and thinly slice onions for even pickling.
2. **Combine pickling ingredients:** In a large pot, mix vinegar, sugar, salt, turmeric, mustard seeds, celery seeds, ground cloves, and water. Stir until sugar and salt dissolve.
3. **Heat mixture:** Simmer over medium heat, stirring occasionally.
4. **Add onions:** Add sliced onions to the pot and stir to submerge in the liquid.
5. **Simmer onions:** Simmer for 5-8 minutes until just tender.
6. **Sterilize jars:** While onions simmer, sterilize jars and lids by boiling for 10 minutes.
7. **Pack jars:** Ladle onions and liquid into jars, leaving 1/2 inch (12 mm) headspace. Remove air bubbles.
8. **Seal jars:** Wipe rims clean, place lids, and screw bands fingertip tight.
9. **Process in water bath:** Boil jars in water bath for 10 minutes, adjusting for altitude if needed.
10. **Cool and store:** Cool jars for 12-24 hours. Check seals by pressing the lid center. Store in a cool, dark place.

ADDITIONAL TIPS:

- For a spicier version, add a few dried chili flakes to the pickling liquid.
- If you prefer a sweeter taste, you can increase the sugar up to 1 1/4 cups (about 250 grams).

TESTING AND CHECKING THE RECIPE:

- To test the flavor and doneness of the onions before canning, remove a slice and let it cool. Adjust the seasoning if necessary.

STORAGE:

- Store jars in a cool, dark place. Properly sealed, the pickled onions should last up to 1 year. Once opened, refrigerate and use within a month.

CURRIED PICKLED CARROTS

- ◆ 2 lbs (about 0.9 kg) carrots, peeled and sliced diagonally
- ◆ 2 cups (about 480 ml) water
- ◆ 2 cups (about 480 ml) apple cider vinegar
- ◆ 1/4 cup (about 50 grams) sugar
- ◆ 2 tablespoons (about 30 grams) curry powder
- ◆ 1 tablespoon (about 15 grams) salt
- ◆ 1 teaspoon (about 2 grams) mustard seeds
- ◆ 1/2 teaspoon (about 1 gram) turmeric
- ◆ 4 garlic cloves, peeled
- ◆ 4 clean pint-sized (about 473 ml) canning jars with lids and bands

INSTRUCTIONS:

1. **Prepare carrots:** Wash, peel, and slice carrots diagonally into 1/4 inch (6 mm) pieces.
2. **Sterilize jars:** Boil jars and lids for 10 minutes to sterilize. Keep hot until ready to use.
3. **Make pickling liquid:** In a large pot, combine water, vinegar, sugar, curry powder, salt, mustard seeds, and turmeric. Bring to a boil, stirring until dissolved.
4. **Add carrots to liquid:** Add carrots to the boiling liquid and cook for 2-3 minutes.
5. **Pack jars:** Use tongs to place carrots into jars. Add one garlic clove to each jar.
6. **Fill jars with liquid:** Ladle hot pickling liquid into jars, leaving 1/2 inch (12 mm) headspace.
7. **Remove air bubbles:** Stir gently to remove air bubbles using a non-metallic tool.
8. **Seal jars:** Wipe rims clean, place lids, and screw bands fingertip tight.
9. **Process in water bath:** Boil jars in water bath for 15 minutes, adjusting for altitude if necessary.
10. **Cool and store:** Cool jars for 12-24 hours. Check seals by pressing the lid center. Store in a cool, dark place.

ADDITIONAL TIPS:

- ◆ For a spicier variation, add a small dried chili pepper to each jar before adding the carrots.
- ◆ If you prefer a sweeter pickle, you can increase the sugar up to 1/2 cup (about 100 grams).

TESTING AND CHECKING THE RECIPE:

- ◆ To ensure the carrots have the right flavor and texture, let them sit in the sealed jars for at least 2 weeks before opening. This waiting period allows the flavors to meld and develop.

STORAGE:

- ◆ Store jars in a cool, dark place. Properly sealed, the pickled carrots should last up to 1 year. Once opened, refrigerate and use within a month.

PICKLED GREEN BEANS IN BRINE

INGREDIENTS:

- 2 lbs (about 0.9 kg) fresh green beans, ends trimmed
- 4 cups (about 950 ml) water
- 2 cups (about 475 ml) white vinegar
- 2 tablespoons (about 30 grams) pickling salt
- 4 cloves garlic, peeled and halved
- 4 teaspoons (about 20 grams) dill seeds
- 2 teaspoons (about 10 grams) mustard seeds
- 1 teaspoon (about 5 grams) red pepper flakes (optional for heat)
- 4 clean pint-sized (about 473 ml) canning jars with lids and bands

INSTRUCTIONS:

1. **Sterilize jars:** Boil jars and lids for 10 minutes. Keep hot until ready to use.
2. **Prepare green beans:** Wash beans, trim ends, and cut to fit jar height if needed.
3. **Make brine:** In a large pot, combine water, vinegar, and pickling salt. Bring to a boil, stirring until dissolved.
4. **Pack jars:** Add garlic, dill seeds, mustard seeds, and red pepper flakes (optional) to each jar. Pack beans vertically, leaving 1/2 inch (12 mm) headspace.
5. **Fill jars with brine:** Ladle hot brine into jars, leaving 1/2 inch headspace. Remove air bubbles.
6. **Seal jars:** Wipe rims clean, place lids, and screw bands fingertip tight.
7. **Process in water bath:** Boil jars in water bath for 10 minutes, adjusting for altitude if needed.
8. **Cool and store:** Cool jars for 12-24 hours. Check seals by pressing the lid center. Store in a cool, dark place.

ADDITIONAL TIPS:

- For crisper pickled green beans, add a grape leaf to each jar before adding the beans.
- Experiment with other spices such as black peppercorns or coriander seeds for different flavors.

TESTING AND CHECKING THE RECIPE:

- To check if the jars have sealed, press down on the center of the lid after cooling. If the lid doesn't move, the jar is sealed.

STORAGE:

- Store jars in a cool, dark place. Properly sealed, the pickled green beans should last up to 1 year. Once opened, refrigerate and use within a month.

MINT ZUCCHINI PICKLES

INGREDIENTS:

- ♦ 2 lbs (about 0.9 kg) zucchini, sliced into 1/4 inch (about 6 mm) rounds
- ♦ 2 cups (about 475 ml) water
- ♦ 2 cups (about 475 ml) white vinegar
- ♦ 2 tablespoons (about 30 grams) pickling salt
- ♦ 1 tablespoon (about 15 grams) sugar
- ♦ 4 cloves garlic, peeled and lightly crushed
- ♦ 2 teaspoons (about 10 grams) black peppercorns
- ♦ 4 fresh mint sprigs
- ♦ 4 clean pint-sized (about 473 ml) canning jars with lids and bands

INSTRUCTIONS:

1. **Prepare zucchini:** Wash and slice zucchini into 1/4 inch rounds for even pickling.
2. **Sterilize jars:** Boil jars and lids for 10 minutes to sterilize. Keep hot until ready to use.
3. **Make brine:** In a large pot, combine water, vinegar, salt, and sugar. Heat and stir until dissolved.
4. **Pack jars:** Add garlic, peppercorns, and mint sprig to each jar. Pack zucchini tightly, leaving 1/2 inch (12 mm) headspace.
5. **Fill jars with brine:** Ladle hot brine over zucchini, maintaining 1/2 inch headspace. Remove air bubbles.
6. **Seal jars:** Wipe rims clean, place lids, and screw bands fingertip tight.
7. **Process in water bath:** Boil jars in water bath for 10 minutes, adjusting for altitude if necessary.
8. **Cool and store:** Cool jars for 12-24 hours. Check seals by pressing the lid center. Store in a cool, dark place.

ADDITIONAL TIPS:

- ♦ For a spicier variation, add a small chili pepper or a teaspoon of crushed red pepper flakes to each jar before adding the zucchini.
- ♦ If you prefer a sweeter pickle, increase the sugar in the brine to 2 tablespoons (about 25 grams).

TESTING AND CHECKING THE RECIPE:

- ♦ To ensure the zucchini pickles have the right flavor and texture, let them sit in the sealed jars for at least 2 weeks before opening. This allows the flavors to meld and develop.

STORAGE:

- ♦ Store jars in a cool, dark place. Properly sealed, the zucchini pickles should last up to 1 year. Once opened, refrigerate and consume within a month.

CAULIFLOWER WITH TURMERIC

INGREDIENTS:

- 2 lbs (about 0.9 kg) cauliflower, cut into florets
- 4 cups (about 950 ml) water
- 2 cups (about 475 ml) white vinegar
- 2 tablespoons (about 30 grams) pickling salt
- 1 tablespoon (about 15 grams) turmeric
- 1 teaspoon (about 5 grams) mustard seeds
- 1 teaspoon (about 5 grams) cumin seeds
- 4 cloves garlic, peeled
- 4 clean pint-sized (about 473 ml) canning jars with lids and bands

INSTRUCTIONS:

1. **Sterilize jars:** Boil jars and lids for 10 minutes. Keep hot until ready to use.
2. **Prepare cauliflower:** Wash cauliflower florets thoroughly.
3. **Make pickling liquid:** In a large pot, combine water, vinegar, salt, turmeric, mustard seeds, and cumin seeds. Bring to a boil, stirring to dissolve salt.
4. **Blanch cauliflower:** Add cauliflower to boiling liquid and cook for 2 minutes.
5. **Pack jars:** Use tongs to distribute cauliflower evenly into jars. Add one garlic clove to each jar.
6. **Fill jars with liquid:** Ladle hot pickling liquid over cauliflower, leaving 1/2 inch (12 mm) headspace. Remove air bubbles.
7. **Seal jars:** Wipe rims clean, place lids, and screw bands fingertip tight.
8. **Process in water bath:** Boil jars in a water bath for 10 minutes, adjusting for altitude if needed.
9. **Cool and store:** Cool jars for 12-24 hours. Check seals by pressing the lid center. Store in a cool, dark place.

ADDITIONAL TIPS:

- For a spicier variation, add a few slices of fresh ginger or a teaspoon of crushed red pepper flakes to the pickling liquid.
- If you prefer a sweeter pickle, you can add up to 1 tablespoon (about 12.5 grams) of sugar to the pickling liquid.

TESTING AND CHECKING THE RECIPE:

- To check if the jars have sealed, press down on the center of the lid after cooling. If the lid doesn't move, the jar is sealed.

STORAGE:

- Store jars in a cool, dark place. Properly sealed, the pickled cauliflower should last up to 1 year. Once opened, refrigerate and use within a month.

SPICY RADISHES

INGREDIENTS:

- 2 lbs (about 0.9 kg) radishes, trimmed and halved
- 2 cups (about 475 ml) white vinegar
- 2 cups (about 475 ml) water
- 2 tablespoons (about 30 grams) pickling salt
- 1 tablespoon (about 15 grams) sugar
- 2 teaspoons (about 10 grams) crushed red pepper flakes
- 4 cloves garlic, peeled and sliced
- 1 teaspoon (about 5 grams) mustard seeds
- 4 clean pint-sized (about 473 ml) canning jars with lids and bands

INSTRUCTIONS:

1. **Sterilize jars:** Boil jars and lids for 10 minutes to sterilize. Keep hot until ready to use.
2. **Prepare radishes:** Wash radishes, trim tops and roots, and halve larger ones.
3. **Make pickling liquid:** In a large pot, combine vinegar, water, salt, and sugar. Heat, stirring until dissolved.
4. **Add spices to jars:** Divide red pepper flakes, garlic, and mustard seeds evenly among the jars.
5. **Pack jars with radishes:** Pack radish halves tightly into jars, leaving 1/2 inch (12 mm) headspace.
6. **Fill jars with liquid:** Ladle hot pickling liquid over radishes, leaving 1/2 inch headspace. Remove air bubbles.
7. **Seal jars:** Wipe rims clean, place lids, and screw bands fingertip tight.
8. **Process in water bath:** Boil jars in water bath for 10 minutes, adjusting for altitude if needed.
9. **Cool and store:** Cool jars for 12-24 hours. Check seals by pressing the lid center. Store in a cool, dark place.

ADDITIONAL TIPS:

- For extra heat, you can increase the amount of crushed red pepper flakes up to 1 tablespoon (about 15 grams) per jar.
- Adding a few slices of fresh ginger to each jar can introduce a unique, spicy flavor that complements the radishes well.

TESTING AND CHECKING THE RECIPE:

- To ensure the radishes have the right flavor and texture, let them sit in the sealed jars for at least 2 weeks before opening. This waiting period allows the flavors to meld and develop.

STORAGE:

- Store jars in a cool, dark place. Properly sealed, the pickled radishes should last up to 1 year. Once opened, refrigerate and use within a month.

PICKLED GREEN TOMATOES

INGREDIENTS:

- 2 lbs (about 0.9 kg) green tomatoes, washed and sliced into halves
- 4 cups (about 950 ml) water
- 2 cups (about 475 ml) white vinegar
- 2 tablespoons (about 30 grams) pickling salt
- 1 tablespoon (about 15 grams) sugar
- 4 cloves garlic, peeled
- 2 teaspoons (about 10 grams) mustard seeds
- 2 teaspoons (about 10 grams) black peppercorns
- 1 teaspoon (about 5 grams) celery seeds
- 4 clean pint-sized (about 473 ml) canning jars with lids and bands

INSTRUCTIONS:

1. **Sterilize jars:** Boil jars and lids for 10 minutes to sterilize. Keep hot until ready to use.
2. **Prepare tomatoes:** Wash and slice green tomatoes into halves or quarters.
3. **Make pickling liquid:** In a large pot, combine water, vinegar, salt, and sugar. Heat and stir until dissolved.
4. **Add spices to jars:** Divide garlic, mustard seeds, peppercorns, and celery seeds evenly among jars.
5. **Pack jars:** Tightly pack tomato halves into jars, leaving 1/2 inch (12 mm) headspace.
6. **Fill jars with liquid:** Ladle hot pickling liquid over tomatoes, leaving 1/2 inch headspace. Remove air bubbles.
7. **Seal jars:** Wipe rims clean, place lids, and screw bands fingertip tight.
8. **Process in water bath:** Boil jars in water bath for 15 minutes, adjusting for altitude if necessary.
9. **Cool and store:** Cool jars for 12-24 hours. Check seals by pressing the lid center. Store in a cool, dark place.

ADDITIONAL TIPS:

- For a spicier variation, add a small chili pepper or a teaspoon of crushed red pepper flakes to each jar before adding the green tomatoes.
- Experiment with other spices such as dill seeds or coriander seeds for different flavors.

TESTING AND CHECKING THE RECIPE:

- To check if the jars have sealed, press down on the center of the lid after cooling. If the lid doesn't move, the jar is sealed.

STORAGE:

- Store jars in a cool, dark place. Properly sealed, the pickled green tomatoes should last up to 1 year. Once opened, refrigerate and use within a month.

PICKLED EGGPLANT

INGREDIENTS:

- ♦ 2 lbs (about 0.9 kg) eggplants, sliced into 1/2 inch (about 1.3 cm) rounds
- ♦ 4 cups (about 950 ml) water
- ♦ 2 cups (about 475 ml) white vinegar
- ♦ 2 tablespoons (about 30 grams) pickling salt
- ♦ 1 tablespoon (about 15 grams) sugar
- ♦ 4 cloves garlic, peeled and sliced
- ♦ 2 teaspoons (about 10 grams) black peppercorns
- ♦ 1 teaspoon (about 5 grams) coriander seeds
- ♦ 4 sprigs fresh dill
- ♦ 4 clean pint-sized (about 473 ml) canning jars with lids and bands

INSTRUCTIONS:

1. **Prepare eggplants:** Wash and slice eggplants into 1/2 inch rounds. Soak in salted water for 1 hour, then drain and pat dry.
2. **Sterilize jars:** Boil jars and lids for 10 minutes to sterilize. Keep hot until ready to use.
3. **Make brine:** In a large pot, combine water, vinegar, salt, and sugar. Heat and stir until dissolved.
4. **Pack jars:** Place garlic, peppercorns, coriander seeds, and a dill sprig in each jar. Pack eggplant slices tightly, leaving 1/2 inch (12 mm) headspace.
5. **Fill jars with brine:** Ladle hot brine over eggplants, leaving 1/2 inch headspace. Remove air bubbles.
6. **Seal jars:** Wipe rims clean, place lids, and screw bands fingertip tight.
7. **Process in water bath:** Boil jars in water bath for 15 minutes, adjusting for altitude if needed.
8. **Cool and store:** Cool jars for 12-24 hours. Check seals by pressing the lid center. Store in a cool, dark place.

ADDITIONAL TIPS:

- ♦ For a spicier variation, add a small chili pepper to each jar before adding the eggplant.
- ♦ Experiment with other herbs such as basil or oregano for different flavors.

TESTING AND CHECKING THE RECIPE:

- ♦ To check if the jars have sealed, press down on the center of the lid after cooling. If the lid doesn't move, the jar is sealed.

STORAGE:

- ♦ Store jars in a cool, dark place. Properly sealed, the pickled eggplants should last up to 1 year. Once opened, refrigerate and use within a month.

VANILLA-POACHED PEACHES

INGREDIENTS:

- ◆ 5 lbs (about 2.3 kg) peaches, ripe but firm
- ◆ 4 cups (about 950 ml) water
- ◆ 2 cups (about 400 grams) granulated sugar
- ◆ 1 vanilla bean, split lengthwise, or 1 tablespoon (15 ml) vanilla extract
- ◆ 6 clean pint-sized (about 473 ml) canning jars with lids and bands

INSTRUCTIONS:

1. **Prepare peaches:** Wash peaches and blanch by cutting an "x" on the bottom and boiling for 30-60 seconds. Transfer to ice water, then peel, pit, and slice into halves or quarters.
2. **Sterilize jars:** Boil jars and lids for 10 minutes to sterilize. Keep hot until ready to use.
3. **Make syrup:** In a large pot, combine water and sugar. Stir until dissolved, then add vanilla and simmer.
4. **Pack jars:** Pack peeled peaches into jars, leaving 1/2 inch (12 mm) headspace.
5. **Fill jars with syrup:** Ladle hot syrup over peaches, leaving 1/2 inch headspace. Remove air bubbles.
6. **Seal jars:** Wipe rims clean, place lids, and screw bands fingertip tight.
7. **Process in water bath:** Boil jars in water bath for 20 minutes, adjusting for altitude if needed.
8. **Cool and store:** Cool jars for 12-24 hours. Check seals by pressing the lid center. Store in a cool, dark place.

ADDITIONAL TIPS:

- ◆ For a lighter syrup, you can reduce the sugar to 1 cup (about 200 grams). For a heavier syrup, increase the sugar to 3 cups (about 600 grams).
- ◆ You can add a cinnamon stick or a few cloves to the syrup for a spiced variation.

TESTING AND CHECKING THE RECIPE:

- ◆ To ensure the peaches are preserved properly, check the seals on the jars the day after canning. The lids should not flex up and down when the center is pressed.

STORAGE:

- ◆ Store jars in a cool, dark place. Properly sealed, the canned peaches should last up to 1 year. Once opened, refrigerate and consume within a month.

CINNAMON-SYRUP PRUNES

INGREDIENTS:

- 4 lbs (about 1.8 kg) plums, ripe but firm
- 2 cups (about 400 grams) granulated sugar
- 2 cups (about 475 ml) water
- 4 cinnamon sticks
- 6 clean pint-sized (about 473 ml) canning jars with lids and bands

INSTRUCTIONS:

1. **Prepare plums:** Wash, halve, and pit the plums. Quarter if large.
2. **Sterilize jars:** Boil jars and lids for 10 minutes to sterilize. Keep hot until ready to use.
3. **Make syrup:** In a pot, combine water and sugar. Stir until dissolved, add cinnamon sticks, and bring to a simmer.
4. **Cook plums:** Add plums to syrup and simmer for 5 minutes until tender but not falling apart.
5. **Pack jars:** Using a slotted spoon, transfer plums to jars, leaving 1/2 inch (12 mm) headspace. Remove cinnamon sticks.
6. **Fill jars with syrup:** Ladle syrup over plums, maintaining 1/2 inch headspace. Remove air bubbles.
7. **Seal jars:** Wipe rims clean, place lids, and screw bands fingertip tight.
8. **Process in water bath:** Boil jars in water bath for 20 minutes, adjusting for altitude if needed.
9. **Cool and store:** Cool jars for 12-24 hours. Check seals by pressing the lid center. Store in a cool, dark place.

ADDITIONAL TIPS:

- For a spicier variation, add a few cloves or a star anise to the syrup while cooking.
- If you prefer a sweeter syrup, you can increase the sugar to 3 cups (about 600 grams).

TESTING AND CHECKING THE RECIPE:

- To ensure the plums are preserved properly, check the seals on the jars the day after canning. The lids should not flex up and down when the center is pressed.

STORAGE:

- Store jars in a cool, dark place. Properly sealed, the canned plums should last up to 1 year. Once opened, refrigerate and consume within a month.

ALMOND-SYRUP CHERRIES

- 4 lbs (about 1.8 kg) cherries, pitted
- 2 cups (about 400 grams) granulated sugar
- 3 cups (about 710 ml) water
- 1 cup (about 240 ml) almond liqueur
- 6 clean pint-sized (about 473 ml) canning jars with lids and bands

INSTRUCTIONS:

1. **Prepare cherries:** Wash and pit cherries, keeping them whole for better presentation.
2. **Sterilize jars:** Boil jars and lids for 10 minutes to sterilize. Keep hot until ready to use.
3. **Make syrup:** In a pot, combine water and sugar. Stir until dissolved, simmer for 5 minutes to create a light syrup.
4. **Add liqueur:** Remove syrup from heat and stir in almond liqueur.
5. **Pack jars:** Pack cherries tightly into jars, leaving 1/2 inch (12 mm) headspace.
6. **Fill jars with syrup:** Ladle syrup over cherries, maintaining 1/2 inch headspace. Remove air bubbles.
7. **Seal jars:** Wipe rims clean, place lids, and screw bands fingertip tight.
8. **Process in water bath:** Boil jars in water bath for 25 minutes, adjusting for altitude if needed.
9. **Cool and store:** Cool jars for 12-24 hours. Check seals by pressing the lid center. Store in a cool, dark place.

ADDITIONAL TIPS:

- If you prefer a non-alcoholic version, substitute the almond liqueur with almond extract. Use 2 tablespoons (about 30 ml) of almond extract mixed with 1 cup (about 240 ml) of water as a replacement.
- For a spicier twist, add a cinnamon stick or a few cloves to each jar before adding the cherries.

TESTING AND CHECKING THE RECIPE:

- To ensure the cherries are preserved properly, check the seals on the jars the day after canning. The lids should not flex up and down when the center is pressed.

STORAGE:

- Store jars in a cool, dark place. Properly sealed, the canned cherries should last up to 1 year. Once opened, refrigerate and consume within a month.

CARAMELIZED APPLES

INGREDIENTS:

- 6 lbs (about 2.7 kg) apples, firm and tart variety (e.g., Granny Smith)
- 4 cups (about 950 ml) water
- 2 cups (about 400 grams) granulated sugar
- 1 cup (about 240 ml) caramel syrup
- 2 teaspoons (about 10 ml) vanilla extract
- 6 cinnamon sticks
- 6 clean pint-sized (about 473 ml) canning jars with lids and bands

INSTRUCTIONS:

1. **Prepare apples:** Wash, peel, core, and slice apples into wedges or rings.
2. **Sterilize jars:** Boil jars and lids for 10 minutes to sterilize. Keep hot until ready to use.
3. **Make syrup:** In a pot, combine water, sugar, caramel syrup, and vanilla. Stir until dissolved, then simmer.
4. **Cook apples:** Add apple slices to syrup and simmer for 5 minutes until just tender.
5. **Pack jars:** Transfer apple slices into jars, leaving 1/2 inch (12 mm) headspace. Add one cinnamon stick to each jar.
6. **Fill jars with syrup:** Ladle hot syrup over apples, maintaining 1/2 inch headspace. Remove air bubbles.
7. **Seal jars:** Wipe rims clean, place lids, and screw bands fingertip tight.
8. **Process in water bath:** Boil jars in water bath for 20 minutes, adjusting for altitude if needed.
9. **Cool and store:** Cool jars for 12-24 hours. Check seals by pressing the lid center. Store in a cool, dark place.

ADDITIONAL TIPS:

- For a richer flavor, you can add a splash of rum or brandy to the syrup.
- If you prefer a less sweet version, reduce the sugar to 1 cup (about 200 grams).

TESTING AND CHECKING THE RECIPE:

- To ensure the apples are preserved properly, check the seals on the jars the day after canning. The lids should not flex up and down when the center is pressed.

STORAGE:

- Store jars in a cool, dark place. Properly sealed, the canned caramel apples should last up to 1 year. Once opened, refrigerate and consume within a month.

GINGER-POACHED PEARS

INGREDIENTS:

- 6 lbs (about 2.7 kg) pears, ripe but firm
- 2 cups (about 400 grams) granulated sugar
- 4 cups (about 950 ml) water
- 2 tablespoons (about 30 ml) fresh lemon juice
- 4 inches (about 10 cm) fresh ginger, peeled and thinly sliced
- 6 clean pint-sized (about 473 ml) canning jars with lids and bands

INSTRUCTIONS:

1. **Prepare pears:** Wash, peel, core, and cut pears into halves or quarters.
2. **Sterilize jars:** Boil jars and lids for 10 minutes to sterilize. Keep hot until ready to use.
3. **Make syrup:** In a pot, combine sugar, water, and lemon juice. Stir until dissolved, add ginger, and bring to a simmer.
4. **Cook pears:** Add pears to syrup and simmer for 5 minutes until just tender.
5. **Pack jars:** Transfer pears into jars, leaving 1/2 inch (12 mm) headspace. Divide ginger slices among jars.
6. **Fill jars with syrup:** Ladle syrup over pears, maintaining 1/2 inch headspace. Remove air bubbles.
7. **Seal jars:** Wipe rims clean, place lids, and screw bands fingertip tight.
8. **Process in water bath:** Boil jars in water bath for 20 minutes, adjusting for altitude if needed.
9. **Cool and store:** Cool jars for 12-24 hours. Check seals by pressing the lid center. Store in a cool, dark place.

ADDITIONAL TIPS:

- For a spicier variation, add a few peppercorns or a cinnamon stick to each jar before adding the pears.
- If you prefer a less sweet syrup, you can reduce the sugar to 1 cup (about 200 grams).

TESTING AND CHECKING THE RECIPE:

- To ensure the pears are preserved properly, check the seals on the jars the day after canning. The lids should not flex up and down when the center is pressed.

STORAGE:

- Store jars in a cool, dark place. Properly sealed, the canned pears should last up to 1 year. Once opened, refrigerate and consume within a month.

SPECIAL SECTION: CANNING MEATS AND PROTEINS

RED MEAT

BEEF IN TOMATO SAUCE

INGREDIENTS:

- 3 lbs (about 1.36 kg) beef chuck, cut into 1-inch cubes
- 2 tablespoons (about 30 ml) olive oil
- 1 large onion, finely chopped
- 4 cloves garlic, minced
- 2 cups (about 480 ml) beef broth
- 1 can (28 oz or about 794 grams) crushed tomatoes
- 2 tablespoons (about 30 ml) tomato paste
- 1 teaspoon (about 5 ml) salt
- 1/2 teaspoon (about 2.5 ml) black pepper
- 1 teaspoon (about 5 ml) dried oregano
- 1 teaspoon (about 5 ml) dried basil
- 6 clean pint-sized (about 473 ml) canning jars with lids and bands

INSTRUCTIONS:

1. **Brown beef:** Heat olive oil in a skillet. Brown beef in batches, then set aside.
2. **Sauté vegetables:** In the same skillet, sauté onion and garlic until soft.
3. **Combine beef and vegetables:** Return beef to the skillet. Add broth, tomatoes, tomato paste, salt, pepper, oregano, and basil. Stir to combine.
4. **Simmer:** Cover and simmer on low heat for 1.5 to 2 hours until beef is tender.
5. **Sterilize jars:** While beef simmers, boil jars and lids for 10 minutes to sterilize.
6. **Fill jars:** Ladle beef mixture into jars, leaving 1 inch (25 mm) headspace. Remove air bubbles.
7. **Seal jars:** Wipe rims clean, place lids, and screw bands fingertip tight.
8. **Process in water bath:** Boil jars in water bath for 90 minutes, adjusting for altitude if needed.
9. **Cool and store:** Cool jars for 12-24 hours. Check seals by pressing the lid center. Store in a cool, dark place.

ADDITIONAL TIPS:

- Add red pepper flakes for a spicier version.
- Simmer uncovered for the last 30 minutes if you prefer a thicker sauce.

TESTING AND CHECKING THE RECIPE:

- To ensure the beef is preserved properly, check the seals on the jars the day after canning. The lids should not flex up and down when the center is pressed.

STORAGE:

- Store jars in a cool, dark place. Properly sealed, the canned beef in tomato sauce should last up to 1 year. Once opened, refrigerate and consume within a week.

VEAL STEW WITH VEGETABLES

INGREDIENTS:

- ◆ 3 lbs (about 1.36 kg) veal stew meat, cut into 1-inch cubes
- ◆ 2 tablespoons (about 30 ml) olive oil
- ◆ 1 large onion, diced
- ◆ 3 cloves garlic, minced
- ◆ 2 carrots, peeled and sliced
- ◆ 2 stalks celery, sliced
- ◆ 1 cup (about 240 ml) dry white wine
- ◆ 1 can (14.5 oz or about 411 grams) diced tomatoes
- ◆ 1 cup (about 240 ml) beef broth
- ◆ 1 teaspoon (about 5 ml) salt
- ◆ 1/2 teaspoon (about 2.5 ml) black pepper
- ◆ 1 teaspoon (about 5 ml) dried thyme
- ◆ 1 bay leaf
- ◆ 6 clean pint-sized (about 473 ml) canning jars with lids and bands

INSTRUCTIONS:

1. **Brown veal:** Heat olive oil in a skillet, brown veal in batches, then set aside.
2. **Sauté vegetables:** In the same skillet, sauté onion, garlic, carrots, and celery until soft (5-7 minutes).
3. **Deglaze with wine:** Add wine, scraping up browned bits, and simmer until reduced by half (3-4 minutes).
4. **Combine ingredients:** Add veal, tomatoes, broth, salt, pepper, thyme, and bay leaf. Stir to combine.
5. **Simmer:** Cover and simmer on low for 1.5 to 2 hours until veal is tender.
6. **Sterilize jars:** While stew simmers, boil jars and lids for 10 minutes to sterilize.
7. **Fill jars:** Ladle stew into jars, leaving 1 inch (25 mm) headspace. Remove air bubbles.
8. **Seal jars:** Wipe rims clean, place lids, and screw bands fingertip tight.
9. **Process in water bath:** Boil jars in water bath for 90 minutes, adjusting for altitude if needed.
10. **Cool and store:** Cool jars for 12-24 hours. Check seals by pressing the lid center. Store in a cool, dark place.

ADDITIONAL TIPS:

- ◆ Y Add potatoes or mushrooms for a heartier stew during the last 30 minutes of simmering.
- ◆ For a richer flavor, you can sear the veal with a sprinkle of flour before browning. This will also help thicken the stew.

TESTING AND CHECKING THE RECIPE:

- ◆ To ensure the veal stew is preserved properly, check the seals on the jars the day after canning. The lids should not flex up and down when the center is pressed.

STORAGE:

- ◆ Store jars in a cool, dark place. Properly sealed, the canned veal stew should last up to 1 year. Once opened, refrigerate and consume within a week.

MEAT RAGU'

INGREDIENTS:

- ◆ 3 lbs (about 1.36 kg) ground beef
- ◆ 1 large onion, diced (about 1 cup or 240 ml)
- ◆ 4 cloves garlic, minced
- ◆ 2 cans (28 oz or about 794 grams each) crushed tomatoes
- ◆ 1 can (6 oz or about 170 grams) tomato paste
- ◆ 1 cup (about 240 ml) beef broth
- ◆ 1/2 cup (about 120 ml) red wine (optional)
- ◆ 2 tablespoons (about 30 ml) olive oil
- ◆ 1 teaspoon (about 5 ml) salt
- ◆ 1/2 teaspoon (about 2.5 ml) black pepper
- ◆ 1 teaspoon (about 5 ml) dried oregano
- ◆ 1 teaspoon (about 5 ml) dried basil
- ◆ 6 clean pint-sized (about 473 ml) canning jars with lids and bands

INSTRUCTIONS:

1. **Cook ground beef:** Heat olive oil in a skillet, add beef, and cook until browned. Drain excess fat.
2. **Sauté onion and garlic:** Add onion to the beef and cook until soft. Stir in garlic and cook for 1 minute.
3. **Add tomatoes and seasonings:** Stir in crushed tomatoes, tomato paste, broth, red wine (optional), salt, pepper, oregano, and basil. Bring to a simmer.
4. **Simmer ragù:** Reduce heat and simmer uncovered for 1-2 hours, stirring occasionally, until thickened.
5. **Sterilize jars:** While the ragù simmers, boil jars and lids for 10 minutes to sterilize.
6. **Fill jars:** Ladle hot ragù into jars, leaving 1 inch (25 mm) headspace. Remove air bubbles.
7. **Seal jars:** Wipe rims clean, place lids, and screw bands fingertip tight.
8. **Process in water bath:** Boil jars in water bath for 90 minutes, adjusting for altitude if needed.
9. **Cool and store:** Cool jars for 12-24 hours. Check seals by pressing the lid center. Store in a cool, dark place.

ADDITIONAL TIPS:

- ◆ For a richer flavor, you can add 1/2 cup (about 120 ml) of grated Parmesan cheese to the ragù during the last 15 minutes of simmering.
- ◆ If you prefer a chunkier sauce, consider adding diced bell peppers or mushrooms along with the onions.

TESTING AND CHECKING THE RECIPE:

- ◆ To ensure the ragù is preserved properly, check the seals on the jars the day after canning. The lids should not flex up and down when the center is pressed.

STORAGE:

- ◆ Store jars in a cool, dark place. Properly sealed, the canned ragù should last up to 1 year. Once opened, refrigerate and consume within a week.

CHILI BEEF

INGREDIENTS:

- 3 lbs (about 1.36 kg) beef chuck, cut into 1-inch cubes
- 2 tablespoons (about 30 ml) olive oil
- 1 large onion, chopped
- 4 cloves garlic, minced
- 2 tablespoons (about 30 ml) chili powder
- 1 teaspoon (about 5 ml) cumin
- 1/2 teaspoon (about 2.5 ml) smoked paprika
- 1/4 teaspoon (about 1.25 ml) cayenne pepper (adjust to taste)
- 1 can (28 oz or about 794 grams) diced tomatoes, undrained
- 1/2 cup (about 120 ml) beef broth
- 1 teaspoon (about 5 ml) salt
- 1/2 teaspoon (about 2.5 ml) black pepper
- 6 clean pint-sized (about 473 ml) canning jars with lids and bands

INSTRUCTIONS:

1. **Brown the beef:** Heat olive oil in a skillet over medium-high heat. Brown the beef cubes on all sides for 5-7 minutes. Transfer to a plate.
2. **Sauté the aromatics:** In the same skillet, sauté onion and garlic until soft, about 3-4 minutes.
3. **Add spices:** Return beef to the skillet. Stir in chili powder, cumin, smoked paprika, and cayenne pepper. Cook for 1-2 minutes until fragrant.
4. **Add tomatoes and broth:** Stir in diced tomatoes (with juice) and beef broth. Season with salt and pepper. Bring to a simmer.
5. **Simmer the beef:** Reduce heat to low, cover, and simmer for 1.5-2 hours, or until beef is tender.
6. **Sterilize jars:** While beef simmers, sterilize jars and lids by boiling them for 10 minutes. Keep jars hot until use.
7. **Fill jars:** Ladle hot beef mixture into jars, leaving 1 inch (25 mm) headspace. Remove air bubbles using a non-metallic tool.
8. **Seal the jars:** Wipe jar rims clean, place lids on jars, and screw bands until fingertip tight.
9. **Process in water bath:** Boil jars for 90 minutes, adjusting time for high altitude.
10. **Cool and store:** Cool jars for 12-24 hours, check seals, and store in a cool, dark place.

ADDITIONAL TIPS:

- Reduce cayenne for a milder chili.
- Add beans (kidney or black beans) during the last 30 minutes for a heartier chili.

TESTING AND CHECKING THE RECIPE:

- Check jar seals the day after canning; lids shouldn't flex when pressed.

STORAGE:

- Store sealed jars for up to 1 year. Once opened, refrigerate and use within a week.

BARBECUE PORK

INGREDIENTS:

- ♦ 4 lbs (about 1.8 kg) pork shoulder, cut into 2-inch cubes
- ♦ 2 cups (about 480 ml) barbecue sauce, homemade or store-bought
- ♦ 1 cup (about 240 ml) apple cider vinegar
- ♦ 1/2 cup (about 120 ml) brown sugar
- ♦ 2 tablespoons (about 30 ml) Worcestershire sauce
- ♦ 1 tablespoon (about 15 ml) liquid smoke (optional)
- ♦ 1 teaspoon (about 5 ml) garlic powder
- ♦ 1 teaspoon (about 5 ml) onion powder
- ♦ 1/2 teaspoon (about 2.5 ml) smoked paprika
- ♦ Salt and black pepper to taste
- ♦ 6 clean pint-sized (about 473 ml) canning jars with lids and bands

INSTRUCTIONS:

1. **Season the pork:** Generously season pork cubes with salt and pepper.
2. **Make the sauce:** In a large bowl, mix barbecue sauce, vinegar, brown sugar, Worcestershire sauce, liquid smoke (if using), garlic powder, onion powder, and smoked paprika.
3. **Marinate the pork:** Add seasoned pork to the sauce, coat well, and marinate for at least 2 hours in the refrigerator (or overnight for more flavor).
4. **Cook the pork:** Transfer the pork and sauce to a large pot, bring to a simmer over medium heat, reduce to low, and cook for 2-3 hours until pork is tender and shreds easily.
5. **Shred the pork:** Remove pork from the pot, shred with two forks, then return to the sauce and stir to combine.
6. **Sterilize the jars:** While the pork cooks, sterilize jars and lids by boiling them for 10 minutes. Keep them hot until use.
7. **Fill the jars:** Ladle the shredded pork and sauce into hot jars, leaving 1 inch (25 mm) headspace. Remove air bubbles by stirring gently inside the jars with a non-metallic tool.
8. **Seal the jars:** Wipe the rims clean, place lids on jars, and screw on the bands until fingertip tight.
9. **Process in a water bath:** Submerge jars in a boiling water bath and process for 90 minutes. Adjust time for high altitude if needed.
10. **Cool and store:** Let jars cool for 12-24 hours. Check seals by pressing the lid center—if it doesn't pop back, it's sealed. Store in a cool, dark place.

ADDITIONAL TIPS:

- ♦ For spicier pork, add 1 tsp of chili powder or a few dashes of hot sauce to the sauce.
- ♦ For a thicker sauce, simmer the pork uncovered for the last 30 minutes of cooking.

TESTING AND CHECKING THE RECIPE:

- ♦ To ensure the pork is preserved properly, check the seals on the jars the day after canning. The lids should not flex up and down when the center is pressed.

STORAGE:

- ♦ Store sealed jars in a cool, dark place for up to 1 year. Once opened, refrigerate and use within a week.

ROSEMARY LAMB

- 3 lbs (about 1.36 kg) lamb shoulder, cut into 2-inch cubes
- 2 tablespoons (about 30 ml) olive oil
- 4 cloves garlic, minced
- 2 tablespoons (about 30 ml) fresh rosemary, chopped
- 1 teaspoon (about 5 ml) salt
- 1/2 teaspoon (about 2.5 ml) black pepper
- 1 cup (about 240 ml) red wine
- 1/2 cup (about 120 ml) beef broth
- 6 clean pint-sized (about 473 ml) canning jars with lids and bands

INSTRUCTIONS:

1. **Prepare the lamb:** In a large bowl, toss the lamb cubes with olive oil, garlic, rosemary, salt, and black pepper until evenly coated.
2. **Brown the lamb:** Heat a large skillet over medium-high heat. Sear the lamb cubes on all sides in batches until browned. Set the lamb aside.
3. **Deglaze the skillet:** Add red wine to the skillet, scraping up the browned bits with a wooden spoon. Simmer until the wine reduces by half, about 5 minutes.
4. **Simmer the lamb:** Return the lamb to the skillet and add beef broth. Bring to a simmer, reduce the heat to low, cover, and cook for 1.5 to 2 hours until tender.
5. **Prepare the jars:** Sterilize the jars and lids by boiling them for at least 10 minutes. Keep them hot until ready to use.
6. **Fill the jars:** Ladle the hot lamb mixture into the jars, leaving 1 inch (25 mm) headspace. Remove any air bubbles with a non-metallic tool.
7. **Seal the jars:** Wipe the rims with a damp cloth, place the lids on, and screw on the bands until fingertip tight.
8. **Process in a water bath:** Submerge the jars in a boiling water bath and process for 90 minutes. Adjust the time for high altitudes if needed.
9. **Cool and store:** Let the jars cool for 12-24 hours. Check the seals by pressing down in the center—if the lid doesn't pop back, it's sealed. Store the sealed jars in a cool, dark place.

ADDITIONAL TIPS:

- Marinate the lamb with garlic, rosemary, olive oil, salt, and pepper for 2+ hours or overnight.
- To thicken the sauce, add 1 tbsp cornstarch mixed with 2 tbsp water in the last 30 minutes.

TESTING AND CHECKING THE RECIPE:

- To ensure the lamb is preserved properly, check the seals on the jars the day after canning. The lids should not flex up and down when the center is pressed.

STORAGE:

- Store jars in a cool, dark place up to 1 year. Refrigerate and use within a week after opening.

BRESAOLA IN OLIVE OIL

INGREDIENTS:

- 2 lbs (about 0.9 kg) bresaola, thinly sliced
- 4 cups (about 960 ml) extra virgin olive oil
- 4 cloves garlic, peeled and lightly crushed
- 2 tablespoons (about 30 ml) black peppercorns
- 4 sprigs fresh rosemary
- 6 clean pint-sized (about 473 ml) canning jars with lids and bands

INSTRUCTIONS:

1. **Sterilize the jars and lids:** Boil the canning jars and lids for at least 10 minutes to sterilize. Keep them hot until you're ready to use them.
2. **Prepare the bresaola:** Ensure the bresaola slices are intact. Cut them if necessary to fit into the jars.
3. **Layer the bresaola in jars:** Layer the bresaola slices into the jars. Between each layer, add a garlic clove, a few peppercorns, and a sprig of rosemary. Leave about 1 inch (25 mm) of headspace.
4. **Add olive oil:** Pour the olive oil over the bresaola until it is fully submerged. Maintain the 1 inch headspace.
5. **Remove air bubbles:** Use a non-metallic tool to stir inside the jars to release air bubbles. Add more olive oil if needed to cover the bresaola.
6. **Seal the jars:** Wipe the rims of the jars with a damp cloth. Place the lids on and screw the bands until fingertip tight.
7. **Process in a water bath:** Submerge the jars in a boiling water bath and process for 90 minutes. Adjust for altitude if necessary.
8. **Cool and store:** Let the jars cool for 12-24 hours. Check the seals by pressing down in the center of the lid—if the lid doesn't pop back, it's sealed. Store sealed jars in a cool, dark place.

ADDITIONAL TIPS:

- For a more aromatic flavor, you can add a bay leaf or a small piece of lemon peel to each jar.
- Ensure the olive oil covers the bresaola completely to prevent exposure to air, which can lead to spoilage.

TESTING AND CHECKING THE RECIPE:

- After cooling, check the seals on the jars by pressing down in the center of the lid. If the lid doesn't move, the jar is properly sealed.
- If a jar hasn't sealed properly, refrigerate it and consume the bresaola within 2 weeks.

STORAGE:

- Store the sealed jars in a cool, dark place. Properly sealed, the bresaola in olive oil should last up to 1 year. Once opened, refrigerate and use within 1 month for the best quality.

SPICY SAUSAGES

INGREDIENTS:

- 2 lbs (about 0.9 kg) Italian sausage links
- 2 cups (about 480 ml) spicy tomato sauce, homemade or store-bought
- 1 cup (about 240 ml) water
- 1 tablespoon (about 15 ml) olive oil
- 1 teaspoon (about 5 ml) red pepper flakes (adjust to taste)
- 1/2 teaspoon (about 2.5 ml) garlic powder
- 1/2 teaspoon (about 2.5 ml) onion powder
- 6 clean pint-sized (about 473 ml) canning jars with lids and bands

INSTRUCTIONS:

1. **Prepare the sausage:** Prick sausages all over with a fork to prevent them from bursting during cooking.
2. **Brown the sausage:** In a large skillet, heat the olive oil over medium heat. Brown the sausages on all sides for 5-7 minutes. Remove from skillet and set aside.
3. **Combine sauce and spices:** In the same skillet, mix the spicy tomato sauce, water, red pepper flakes, garlic powder, and onion powder. Bring to a simmer.
4. **Cook the sausage in sauce:** Return the sausages to the skillet. Cover and simmer for about 20 minutes, turning them halfway through.
5. **Sterilize the jars and lids:** Boil the jars and lids in water for at least 10 minutes to sterilize. Keep them hot until ready to use.
6. **Fill the jars:** Cut sausages into pieces if necessary to fit into the jars. Divide the sausages among the hot jars, then ladle the sauce over them, leaving 1 inch (25 mm) headspace.
7. **Remove air bubbles:** Use a non-metallic tool to gently stir inside the jars to remove any air bubbles. Adjust the headspace if necessary by adding more sauce.
8. **Seal the jars:** Wipe the rims with a damp cloth, place the lids on, and screw on the bands until fingertip tight.
9. **Process in a water bath:** Submerge the jars in a boiling water bath and process for 90 minutes. Adjust for altitude if needed.
10. **Cool and store:** Let the jars cool for 12-24 hours. Check seals by pressing down on the center of the lids—if the lids don't pop back, they are sealed. Store the sealed jars in a cool, dark place.

ADDITIONAL TIPS:

- For a milder version, reduce the amount of red pepper flakes or use a less spicy tomato sauce.
- You can add a teaspoon of Italian seasoning to the sauce for an extra layer of flavor.

TESTING AND CHECKING THE RECIPE:

- Check jar seals the day after canning; lids shouldn't flex when pressed.

STORAGE:

- Store jars in a cool, dark place for up to 1 year. Once opened, refrigerate and use within a week.

ORANGE CHICKEN

INGREDIENTS:

- 4 lbs (about 1.8 kg) chicken thighs, bone-in and skin-on
- 2 tablespoons (about 30 ml) olive oil
- Salt and pepper, to taste
- 1 cup (about 240 ml) orange juice, freshly squeezed
- 1/4 cup (about 60 ml) lemon juice, freshly squeezed
- 1/4 cup (about 60 ml) honey
- 2 tablespoons (about 30 ml) soy sauce
- 1 tablespoon (about 15 ml) ginger, grated
- 2 cloves garlic, minced
- 1 teaspoon (about 5 ml) orange zest
- 6 clean pint-sized (about 473 ml) canning jars with lids and bands

INSTRUCTIONS:

1. **Preheat oven** to 375°F (190°C) and line a baking sheet with foil.
2. **Pat dry** chicken thighs, **brush with olive oil**, season with salt and pepper, and place on the sheet.
3. **Bake for 35-40 minutes**, until internal temperature reaches 165°F (74°C).
4. In a saucepan, **simmer orange juice**, lemon juice, honey, soy sauce, ginger, garlic, and orange zest for 10-15 minutes, until thickened.
5. **Brush baked chicken** with orange sauce.
6. **Broil for 2-3 minutes**, until sauce caramelizes.
7. While broiling, **sterilize jars and lids** by boiling for 10 minutes.
8. **Cool chicken** slightly, remove skin and bones, cut into bite-sized pieces.
9. **Fill jars** with chicken and sauce, leaving 1 inch (25 mm) headspace.
10. **Stir to remove air bubbles**, adjust headspace.
11. **Wipe rims**, place lids, screw on bands fingertip tight.
12. **Process in boiling water bath** for 75 minutes, adjusting for altitude.
13. **Cool jars for 12-24 hours**, check seals, and store in a cool, dark place.

ADDITIONAL TIPS:

- Add red pepper flakes for a spicy kick.
- Use high-quality store-bought orange juice if fresh is unavailable.

TESTING AND CHECKING THE RECIPE:

- Check seals the next day. Properly sealed lids should not flex when pressed.

STORAGE:

- Store sealed jars in a cool, dark place for up to 1 year. Once opened, refrigerate and use within a week.

AROMATIC TURKEY

INGREDIENTS:

- 4 lbs (about 1.8 kg) turkey breast, boneless and skinless
- 2 tablespoons (about 30 ml) olive oil
- 1 cup (about 240 ml) chicken broth
- 1/4 cup (about 60 ml) white wine vinegar
- 1/4 cup (about 60 ml) fresh lemon juice
- 2 tablespoons (about 30 ml) honey
- 4 cloves garlic, minced
- 2 teaspoons (about 10 ml) dried thyme
- 2 teaspoons (about 10 ml) dried rosemary
- 1 teaspoon (about 5 ml) salt
- 1/2 teaspoon (about 2.5 ml) black pepper
- 6 clean pint-sized (about 473 ml) canning jars with lids and bands

INSTRUCTIONS:

1. **Prepare the turkey:** Cut turkey into 1-inch cubes.
2. **Brown the turkey:** Heat olive oil in a skillet over medium heat. Brown turkey cubes on all sides, 5-7 minutes.
3. **Make the broth:** Mix broth, vinegar, lemon juice, honey, garlic, thyme, rosemary, salt, and pepper.
4. **Cook the turkey:** Add the broth to the skillet, simmer on low for 25-30 minutes until tender.
5. **Sterilize jars:** Boil jars and lids for 10 minutes.
6. **Fill the jars:** Add turkey to the jars, leaving 1 inch of space. Pour hot broth over turkey, maintaining 1-inch headspace.
7. **Remove air bubbles:** Stir to release air bubbles. Adjust liquid if needed.
8. **Seal the jars:** Wipe rims clean, place lids, and tighten bands.
9. **Process in water bath:** Boil jars for 90 minutes. Adjust time for high altitudes.
10. **Cool and store:** Cool for 12-24 hours, check seals. Store in a cool, dark place.

ADDITIONAL TIPS:

- For a richer flavor, you can brown the turkey cubes in batches to ensure they get a nice sear on all sides.
- Feel free to experiment with other herbs like sage or marjoram to create different flavor profiles.

TESTING AND CHECKING THE RECIPE:

- After cooling, check the seals on the jars by pressing down in the center of the lid. If the lid doesn't move, the jar is properly sealed.

STORAGE:

- Store the sealed jars in a cool, dark place. Properly sealed, the aromatic turkey should last up to 1 year. Once opened, refrigerate and consume within a week.

DUCK WITH PROVENAL HERBS

INGREDIENTS:

- 4 duck breasts (about 2 lbs or 0.9 kg)
- 2 tablespoons (30 ml) olive oil
- 1 teaspoon (5 ml) salt
- 1/2 teaspoon (2.5 ml) black pepper
- 1/4 cup (60 ml) dry white wine
- 1/4 cup (60 ml) chicken broth
- 2 tablespoons (30 ml) fresh rosemary, finely chopped
- 2 tablespoons (30 ml) fresh thyme, finely chopped
- 6 clean pint-sized (about 473 ml) canning jars with lids and bands

INSTRUCTIONS:

1. **Prepare the duck:** Pat the duck breasts dry, score the skin in a diamond pattern, and season with salt and pepper.
2. **Sear the duck:** Heat olive oil in a skillet over medium-high. Cook duck skin-side down for 5-7 minutes until crispy, then flip and cook another 4-5 minutes for medium-rare. Set aside to rest.
3. **Make the sauce:** Deglaze the pan with white wine, scraping up any bits. Add broth, rosemary, and thyme. Simmer until reduced by half, about 5 minutes.
4. **Slice the duck:** After resting, slice duck thinly against the grain.
5. **Sterilize jars:** While the sauce reduces, sterilize jars and lids in boiling water for 10 minutes.
6. **Fill the jars:** Divide the duck slices among the jars. Pour the hot herb sauce over the duck, leaving 1-inch headspace.
7. **Remove air bubbles:** Stir gently to remove air bubbles. Adjust headspace if needed.
8. **Seal the jars:** Wipe jar rims clean, place lids, and tighten bands.
9. **Process in water bath:** Submerge jars in boiling water and process for 90 minutes. Adjust time for altitude.
10. **Cool and store:** Cool jars on a towel for 12-24 hours. Check the seals. Store sealed jars in a cool, dark place.

ADDITIONAL TIPS:

- For a richer flavor, consider adding a splash of balsamic vinegar to the sauce.
- If fresh herbs are not available, you can use 1 tablespoon (15 ml) of dried rosemary and thyme, but fresh herbs will provide a better flavor.

TESTING AND CHECKING THE RECIPE:

- To ensure the duck is preserved properly, check the seals on the jars the day after canning. The lids should not flex up and down when the center is pressed.

STORAGE:

- Store jars in a cool, dark place. Properly sealed, the canned duck with herbs should last up to 1 year. Once opened, refrigerate and consume within a week.

CURRIED CHICKEN

INGREDIENTS:

- 4 lbs (about 1.8 kg) chicken thighs, bone-in and skin-on
- 2 tablespoons (about 30 ml) curry powder
- 1 teaspoon (about 5 ml) salt
- 1/2 teaspoon (about 2.5 ml) black pepper
- 1 tablespoon (about 15 ml) olive oil
- 1 large onion, chopped
- 4 cloves garlic, minced
- 1 tablespoon (about 15 ml) ginger, grated
- 1 can (14 oz or about 400 g) diced tomatoes, undrained
- 1 can (13.5 oz or about 400 ml) coconut milk
- 6 clean pint-sized (about 473 ml) canning jars with lids and bands

INSTRUCTIONS:

1. **Season the chicken:** Pat chicken dry, then rub with curry powder, salt, and pepper.
2. **Brown the chicken:** Heat olive oil in a skillet over medium-high. Cook chicken skin-side down for 5-7 minutes until golden, then flip and cook 5 more minutes. Remove from skillet.
3. **Cook the aromatics:** Add onion, garlic, and ginger to the skillet. Cook until softened, about 5 minutes.
4. **Add liquids:** Stir in diced tomatoes and coconut milk. Simmer.
5. **Simmer chicken:** Return chicken to the skillet. Cover and cook for 30 minutes, or until tender.
6. **Sterilize jars:** While chicken cooks, boil jars and lids for 10 minutes to sterilize.
7. **Shred the chicken:** Once done, remove chicken from sauce, cool, then discard skin and bones. Shred the meat.
8. **Fill jars:** Divide shredded chicken among jars. Ladle curry sauce over chicken, leaving 1-inch headspace.
9. **Remove bubbles:** Stir gently to remove air bubbles and adjust headspace as needed.
10. **Seal the jars:** Wipe rims clean, place lids, and tighten bands.
11. **Water bath process:** Submerge jars in boiling water and process for 90 minutes. Adjust time for altitude.
12. **Cool and store:** Let jars cool for 12-24 hours. Check seals. Store in a cool, dark place.

ADDITIONAL TIPS:

- For a spicier curry, add 1 teaspoon (about 5 ml) of cayenne pepper to the curry powder mix.
- If you prefer a thicker sauce, you can mix 1 tablespoon of cornstarch with 2 tablespoons of water and add it to the curry during the last 5 minutes of cooking.

TESTING AND CHECKING THE RECIPE:

- To ensure the chicken curry is preserved properly, check the seals on the jars the day after canning. The lids should not flex up and down when the center is pressed.

STORAGE:

- Store jars in a cool, dark place. Properly sealed, the canned chicken curry should last up to 1 year. Once opened, refrigerate and consume within a week.

GUINEA FOWL WITH OLIVES

INGREDIENTS:

- 4 lbs (about 1.8 kg) guinea fowl, cut into pieces
- 2 tablespoons (about 30 ml) olive oil
- 1 teaspoon (about 5 ml) salt
- 1/2 teaspoon (about 2.5 ml) black pepper
- 1 cup (about 240 ml) dry white wine
- 1 cup (about 240 ml) chicken broth
- 1 cup (about 150 g) pitted green olives
- 4 cloves garlic, minced
- 2 tablespoons (about 30 ml) fresh lemon juice
- 1 tablespoon (about 15 ml) fresh rosemary, chopped
- 6 clean pint-sized (about 473 ml) canning jars with lids and bands

INSTRUCTIONS:

1. **Season the guinea fowl:** Pat dry, then season with salt and pepper.
2. **Brown the meat:** Heat olive oil in a skillet. Brown the guinea fowl on all sides. Set aside.
3. **Deglaze the skillet:** Pour in the wine, scrape up any browned bits, and reduce by half.
4. **Add liquids and seasonings:** Stir in broth, garlic, lemon juice, and rosemary. Bring to a simmer.
5. **Simmer the guinea fowl:** Return the guinea fowl to the skillet, cover, and simmer for 45 minutes until tender.
6. **Add olives:** Stir in olives and cook for 10 more minutes.
7. **Sterilize jars:** Boil jars and lids for 10 minutes to sterilize. Keep warm until ready to use.
8. **Fill jars:** Divide the guinea fowl evenly among the jars. Pour cooking liquid over the meat, leaving 1-inch headspace.
9. **Remove air bubbles:** Gently stir to release bubbles and adjust headspace.
10. **Seal jars:** Wipe rims clean, place lids, and tighten bands.
11. **Water bath process:** Submerge jars in boiling water and process for 90 minutes. Adjust time for altitude if needed.
12. **Cool and store:** Let jars cool for 12-24 hours. Check seals before storing in a cool, dark place.

ADDITIONAL TIPS:

- For a richer flavor, you can add a tablespoon of capers along with the olives.
- Thicken the sauce by mixing 1 tablespoon of flour with water, adding during the last 10 minutes of cooking.

TESTING AND CHECKING THE RECIPE:

- To ensure the guinea fowl is preserved properly, check the seals on the jars the day after canning. The lids should not flex up and down when the center is pressed.

STORAGE:

- Properly sealed, jars last up to 1 year. Once opened, refrigerate and consume within a week.

SPICY CHICKEN WINGS

INGREDIENTS:

- ◆ 3 lbs (about 1.36 kg) chicken wings
- ◆ 1 cup (about 240 ml) hot sauce
- ◆ 1/2 cup (about 120 ml) unsalted butter
- ◆ 2 tablespoons (about 30 ml) apple cider vinegar
- ◆ 1 tablespoon (about 15 ml) Worcestershire sauce
- ◆ 2 teaspoons (about 10 ml) garlic powder
- ◆ 1 teaspoon (about 5 ml) cayenne pepper (adjust to taste)
- ◆ 1 teaspoon (about 5 ml) salt
- ◆ 1/2 teaspoon (about 2.5 ml) black pepper
- ◆ 6 clean pint-sized (about 473 ml) canning jars with lids and bands

INSTRUCTIONS:

1. **Prepare the wings:** Rinse and pat the chicken wings dry. Optionally, cut them at the joints and discard the tips.
2. **Cook the wings:** Preheat oven to 400°F (200°C). Bake wings on a parchment-lined sheet for 45-50 minutes, flipping halfway, until golden and crispy.
3. **Make the sauce:** Combine hot sauce, butter, vinegar, Worcestershire, garlic powder, cayenne, salt, and pepper in a saucepan. Heat on medium, stirring until well combined.
4. **Coat the wings:** Toss cooked wings in the sauce until fully coated.
5. **Sterilize jars:** While the wings are baking, boil jars and lids for 10 minutes. Keep warm until use.
6. **Pack the wings:** Place wings in jars, leaving 1 inch of headspace. Add extra sauce if needed.
7. **Remove air bubbles:** Stir inside jars to release air. Adjust headspace if necessary.
8. **Seal the jars:** Wipe rims clean, place lids, and tighten bands.
9. **Water bath process:** Submerge jars in boiling water and process for 90 minutes. Adjust for altitude if necessary.
10. **Cool and store:** Cool jars for 12-24 hours. Check seals by pressing the lid's center. Store sealed jars in a cool, dark place.

ADDITIONAL TIPS:

- ◆ For a milder sauce, reduce the amount of cayenne pepper or use a milder hot sauce.
- ◆ You can add a tablespoon of honey to the sauce for a sweet and spicy flavor.

TESTING AND CHECKING THE RECIPE:

- ◆ After cooling, press the lid center; if it doesn't move, the jar is sealed.

STORAGE:

- ◆ Properly sealed, jars last up to 1 year. Once opened, refrigerate and consume within a week

LEMON TURKEY

INGREDIENTS:

- ◆ 4 lbs (about 1.8 kg) turkey breast, boneless and skinless
- ◆ 2 tablespoons (about 30 ml) olive oil
- ◆ 1 teaspoon (about 5 ml) salt
- ◆ 1/2 teaspoon (about 2.5 ml) black pepper
- ◆ 1 cup (about 240 ml) chicken broth
- ◆ 1/2 cup (about 120 ml) fresh lemon juice
- ◆ 2 tablespoons (about 30 ml) lemon zest
- ◆ 4 cloves garlic, minced
- ◆ 2 tablespoons (about 30 ml) fresh thyme, chopped
- ◆ 6 clean pint-sized (about 473 ml) canning jars with lids and bands

INSTRUCTIONS:

1. **Prepare the turkey:** Cut turkey into 1-inch cubes and season with salt and pepper.
2. **Brown the turkey:** Heat olive oil in a skillet over medium-high heat. Brown turkey on all sides for about 5-7 minutes.
3. **Make the lemon sauce:** Reduce heat to medium. Add chicken broth, lemon juice, lemon zest, garlic, and thyme. Stir and bring to a simmer.
4. **Cook turkey in the sauce:** Add the turkey back to the skillet. Cover and simmer for 20-25 minutes, until tender.
5. **Sterilize jars:** While cooking, sterilize jars and lids by boiling them for 10 minutes. Keep them hot until ready.
6. **Fill the jars:** Evenly distribute turkey into hot jars. Pour lemon sauce over, leaving 1 inch of headspace.
7. **Remove air bubbles:** Stir inside the jars to release air bubbles. Adjust headspace if necessary.
8. **Seal the jars:** Wipe rims, place lids, and tighten bands fingertip-tight.
9. **Process in a water bath:** Submerge jars in boiling water and process for 90 minutes. Adjust for altitude if needed.
10. **Cool and store:** Cool jars for 12-24 hours. Check seals by pressing the center of the lid. Store sealed jars in a cool, dark place.

ADDITIONAL TIPS:

- ◆ For a more intense lemon flavor, you can add an extra tablespoon of lemon zest.
- ◆ If you prefer a thicker sauce, you can mix 1 tablespoon of cornstarch with 2 tablespoons of water

TESTING AND CHECKING THE RECIPE:

- ◆ Check seals the day after canning; lids shouldn't flex when pressed.

STORAGE:

- ◆ Sealed jars last up to 1 year. Once opened, refrigerate and consume within a week.

HUNTER'S RABBIT

INGREDIENTS:

- 4 lbs (about 1.8 kg) rabbit, cut into pieces
- 2 tablespoons (about 30 ml) olive oil
- 1 teaspoon (about 5 ml) salt
- ½ teaspoon (about 2.5 ml) black pepper
- 1 cup (about 240 ml) dry red wine
- 1 cup (about 240 ml) chicken broth
- 1 can (14 oz or about 400 g) diced tomatoes, undrained
- 1 medium onion, chopped
- 2 cloves garlic, minced
- 1 tablespoon (about 15 ml) fresh rosemary, chopped
- 1 tablespoon (about 15 ml) fresh thyme, chopped
- 6 clean pint-sized (about 473 ml) canning jars with lids and bands

INSTRUCTIONS:

1. **Prepare the rabbit:** Pat dry, then season with salt and pepper.
2. **Brown the rabbit:** Heat olive oil in a skillet over medium-high. Brown rabbit pieces on all sides. Set aside.
3. **Sauté aromatics:** In the same skillet, cook onion and garlic until softened, about 5 minutes.
4. **Deglaze with wine:** Add wine, scraping up browned bits. Simmer and reduce by half, about 5 minutes.
5. **Add broth and tomatoes:** Stir in chicken broth and diced tomatoes. Bring to a simmer.
6. **Return rabbit to skillet:** Add rabbit back to the skillet, sprinkle with rosemary and thyme. Cover and simmer for 1 hour, until tender.
7. **Sterilize jars:** Boil jars and lids for 10 minutes while the rabbit cooks. Keep them hot.
8. **Fill the jars:** Ladle rabbit pieces and cooking liquid into jars, leaving 1 inch headspace.
9. **Remove air bubbles:** Gently stir inside the jars to release air bubbles. Adjust headspace if needed.
10. **Seal the jars:** Wipe rims, place lids, and screw on bands fingertip-tight.
11. **Process in a water bath:** Submerge jars in boiling water and process for 90 minutes. Adjust time for altitude.
12. **Cool and store:** Cool jars for 12-24 hours, check seals, and store in a cool, dark place..

ADDITIONAL TIPS:

- For a richer flavor, you can add a bay leaf or two during the simmering process.
- Thicken the sauce with 1 tbsp of flour mixed with water during the last 10 minutes of cooking.

TESTING AND CHECKING THE RECIPE:

- Check jar seals the next day; lids shouldn't flex when pressed.

STORAGE:

- Properly sealed, jars last up to 1 year. Once opened, refrigerate and consume within a week.

TUNA IN OLIVE OIL

INGREDIENTS:

- ◆ 4 lbs (about 1.8 kg) fresh tuna steaks
- ◆ 4 cups (about 960 ml) olive oil, plus more if needed
- ◆ 4 cloves garlic, peeled and halved
- ◆ 4 bay leaves
- ◆ 1 tablespoon (about 15 ml) whole black peppercorns
- ◆ 1 tablespoon (about 15 ml) kosher salt
- ◆ 6 clean pint-sized (about 473 ml) canning jars with lids and bands

INSTRUCTIONS:

1. **Prepare the tuna:** Cut tuna into pieces that fit in the jars, leaving 1 inch of headspace.
2. **Season the tuna:** Toss the tuna pieces in kosher salt and let sit for 10 minutes.
3. **Pack the jars:** Place 2 garlic halves and 1 bay leaf in each jar. Add tuna, packing tightly. Divide the peppercorns evenly.
4. **Add olive oil:** Pour olive oil over the tuna, fully covering it and leaving 1 inch of headspace. Add more oil if needed.
5. **Remove air bubbles:** Stir gently inside the jars to release air bubbles. Adjust the headspace as needed.
6. **Seal the jars:** Wipe rims, place lids, and screw on the bands until fingertip tight.
7. **Process in a water bath:** Submerge the jars in boiling water and process for 100 minutes. Adjust time for altitude.
8. **Cool and store:** Let jars cool for 12-24 hours. Check the seals by pressing down in the center. If sealed, store in a cool, dark place.

ADDITIONAL TIPS:

- ◆ For a variation in flavor, you can add a sprig of fresh rosemary or thyme to each jar before sealing.
- ◆ Ensure the tuna is completely covered with olive oil in each jar to prevent spoilage.

TESTING AND CHECKING THE RECIPE:

- ◆ After cooling, check the seals on the jars by pressing down in the center of the lid. If the lid doesn't move, the jar is properly sealed.

STORAGE:

- ◆ Store the sealed jars in a cool, dark place. Properly sealed, the canned tuna in olive oil should last up to 1 year. Once opened, refrigerate and consume within a week.

LEMON DILL SALMON

- ◆ 2 lbs (about 0.9 kg) salmon fillets, skin on
- ◆ 2 tablespoons (about 30 ml) olive oil
- ◆ 2 teaspoons (about 10 ml) salt
- ◆ 1 teaspoon (about 5 ml) black pepper
- ◆ 4 lemons, thinly sliced
- ◆ 4 tablespoons (about 60 ml) fresh dill, chopped
- ◆ 1 cup (about 240 ml) white wine
- ◆ 6 clean pint-sized (about 473 ml) canning jars with lids and bands

INSTRUCTIONS:

1. **Prepare the salmon:** Cut the salmon into pieces that fit in the jars, leaving 1 inch of headspace.
2. **Season the salmon:** Mix olive oil, salt, and pepper. Rub on both sides of the salmon.
3. **Layer the jars:** Place lemon slices and dill at the bottom of each sterilized jar. Add salmon pieces, and repeat the layers, finishing with lemon and dill on top.
4. **Add white wine:** Pour white wine into the jars to cover the salmon, leaving 1 inch of headspace.
5. **Remove air bubbles:** Stir inside the jars to release air bubbles and adjust the headspace with more wine if needed.
6. **Seal the jars:** Wipe rims, place lids, and screw on bands until fingertip tight.
7. **Process in a water bath:** Submerge the jars in a boiling water bath for 100 minutes. Adjust time for altitude.
8. **Cool and store:** Let the jars cool for 12-24 hours. Check seals by pressing the lids' center. Store sealed jars in a cool, dark place.

ADDITIONAL TIPS:

- ◆ For a richer flavor, you can add a clove of garlic or a slice of onion to each jar before sealing.
- ◆ Ensure the salmon is completely covered with white wine in each jar to prevent spoilage.

TESTING AND CHECKING THE RECIPE:

- ◆ After cooling, check the seals on the jars by pressing down in the center of the lid. If the lid doesn't move, the jar is properly sealed.

STORAGE:

- ◆ Store the sealed jars in a cool, dark place. Properly sealed, the canned salmon with lemon and dill should last up to 1 year. Once opened, refrigerate and consume within a week.

SMOKED MACKEREL

INGREDIENTS:

- ◆ 2 lbs (about 0.9 kg) mackerel, cleaned and filleted
- ◆ 1 cup (240 ml) soy sauce
- ◆ 1/2 cup (120 ml) water
- ◆ 1/4 cup (60 ml) brown sugar
- ◆ 2 tablespoons (30 ml) liquid smoke
- ◆ 1 tablespoon (15 ml) salt
- ◆ 1 teaspoon (5 ml) garlic powder
- ◆ 1 teaspoon (5 ml) onion powder
- ◆ 6 clean pint-sized (about 473 ml) canning jars with lids and bands

INSTRUCTIONS:

1. **Prepare the brine:** Mix soy sauce, water, brown sugar, liquid smoke, salt, garlic powder, and onion powder until dissolved.
2. **Marinate the mackerel:** Submerge the fillets in the brine, cover, and refrigerate for at least 4 hours or overnight.
3. **Preheat the smoker:** Set your smoker to 175°F (80°C). If using an oven, set it to the lowest temperature with the door slightly open.
4. **Smoke the mackerel:** Pat the fillets dry and smoke for 3-4 hours, or until the internal temperature reaches 145°F (63°C).
5. **Sterilize jars:** Boil the jars and lids for at least 10 minutes to sterilize.
6. **Pack the jars:** Let the smoked mackerel cool slightly, then pack the fillets into the jars, leaving 1 inch of headspace.
7. **Seal the jars:** Wipe the rims clean and place the lids on tightly.
8. **Process in a water bath:** Boil the jars in a water bath for 100 minutes.
9. **Cool and store:** Let the jars cool for 12-24 hours. Check the seals by pressing the lids. Store in a cool, dark place.

ADDITIONAL TIPS:

- ◆ For a spicier kick, add 1 teaspoon (5 ml) of crushed red pepper flakes to the brine.
- ◆ Ensure the mackerel is completely dry before smoking to help the smoke flavor adhere better.

TESTING AND CHECKING THE RECIPE:

- ◆ After cooling, check the seals on the jars by pressing down in the center of the lid. If the lid doesn't move, the jar is properly sealed.

STORAGE:

- ◆ Sealed jars last up to 1 year. Once opened, refrigerate and consume within a week.

MARINARA MUSSELS

INGREDIENTS:

- ♦ 4 lbs (about 1.8 kg) fresh mussels, cleaned and debearded
- ♦ 2 tablespoons (about 30 ml) olive oil
- ♦ 1 large onion, finely chopped
- ♦ 4 cloves garlic, minced
- ♦ 1 cup (240 ml) white wine
- ♦ 1 can (28 oz or about 800 g) diced tomatoes, undrained
- ♦ 1 teaspoon (5 ml) salt
- ♦ 1/2 teaspoon (2.5 ml) black pepper
- ♦ 1/2 teaspoon (2.5 ml) red pepper flakes (optional for heat)
- ♦ 1/4 cup (about 60 ml) fresh parsley, chopped
- ♦ 6 clean pint-sized (about 473 ml) canning jars with lids and bands

INSTRUCTIONS:

1. **Clean the mussels:** Rinse under cold water, scrub shells, and remove beards. Discard any that don't close when tapped.
2. **Cook onion and garlic:** Heat olive oil in a large pot, sauté onion and garlic until softened.
3. **Add mussels:** Increase heat to high, add mussels, cover, and cook for 5 minutes until they start to open.
4. **Add wine and tomatoes:** Pour in wine and tomatoes, season with salt, pepper, and red pepper flakes. Simmer for 5 more minutes. Discard unopened mussels.
5. **Sterilize jars:** Boil jars and lids for 10 minutes.
6. **Pack jars:** Place mussels in jars, then ladle hot broth over, leaving 1 inch headspace.
7. **Seal jars:** Wipe rims, place lids, and screw on bands.
8. **Process in a water bath:** Boil jars for 15 minutes.
9. **Cool and store:** Let jars cool for 12-24 hours, check seals, and store in a cool, dark place.

ADDITIONAL TIPS:

- ♦ Fresh mussels are key for this recipe. Ensure they are fresh by checking that they are closed or close when tapped before cooking.
- ♦ You can add a tablespoon of lemon juice to each jar before sealing for an extra zesty flavor.

TESTING AND CHECKING THE RECIPE:

- ♦ After cooling, check the seals on the jars by pressing down in the center of the lid. If the lid doesn't move, the jar is properly sealed.

STORAGE:

- ♦ Store the sealed jars in a cool, dark place. Properly sealed, the canned mussels in marinara sauce should last up to 1 year. Once opened, refrigerate and consume within 2 days.

TOMATO-BRAISED OCTOPUS

- 2 lbs (about 0.9 kg) octopus, cleaned and tenderized
- 2 tablespoons (30 ml) olive oil
- 1 large onion, finely chopped
- 4 cloves garlic, minced
- 1 can (28 oz or about 800 g) crushed tomatoes
- 1 cup (240 ml) red wine
- 2 bay leaves
- 1 teaspoon (5 ml) salt
- 1/2 teaspoon (2.5 ml) crushed red pepper flakes (optional for heat)
- 1/4 cup (about 60 ml) fresh parsley, chopped
- 6 clean pint-sized (about 473 ml) canning jars with lids and bands

INSTRUCTIONS:

1. **Prep the octopus:** Clean and tenderize the octopus, then cut into 2-inch pieces.
2. **Sauté the aromatics:** Heat olive oil in a large pot, cook onion and garlic until soft.
3. **Brown the octopus:** Add octopus, sauté for 2-3 minutes.
4. **Add tomatoes and wine:** Stir in crushed tomatoes, wine, bay leaves, salt, and red pepper flakes. Simmer.
5. **Cook the octopus:** Cover and simmer on low for 1-1.5 hours, until tender.
6. **Sterilize jars:** Boil jars and lids for 10 minutes while the octopus cooks.
7. **Fill jars:** Remove bay leaves, ladle octopus and sauce into jars, leaving 1 inch headspace.
8. **Remove air bubbles:** Stir to release air bubbles, adjust the headspace if needed.
9. **Seal jars:** Wipe rims clean, place lids, and tighten bands.
10. **Process in water bath:** Boil jars in a water bath for 100 minutes.
11. **Cool and store:** Let jars cool for 12-24 hours. Check seals and store in a cool, dark place.

ADDITIONAL TIPS:

- For a richer flavor, you can add a teaspoon of dried oregano or thyme to the sauce.
- If the octopus is particularly large, increase the cooking time to ensure it becomes tender.

TESTING AND CHECKING THE RECIPE:

- After cooling, check the seals on the jars by pressing down in the center of the lid. If the lid doesn't move, the jar is properly sealed.

STORAGE:

- Store the sealed jars in a cool, dark place. Properly sealed, the canned octopus in tomato sauce should last up to 1 year. Once opened, refrigerate and consume within a week.

CHILI SHRIMP

INGREDIENTS:

- 2 lbs (about 0.9 kg) shrimp, peeled and deveined
- 2 tablespoons (30 ml) olive oil
- 4 cloves garlic, minced
- 1 teaspoon (5 ml) red pepper flakes, more or less to taste
- 1/2 cup (120 ml) white wine
- 1 tablespoon (15 ml) lemon juice
- 1 teaspoon (5 ml) salt
- 1/2 teaspoon (2.5 ml) black pepper
- 6 clean pint-sized (about 473 ml) canning jars with lids and bands

INSTRUCTIONS:

1. **Prepare shrimp:** Clean, peel, and devein the shrimp. Pat dry.
2. **Sauté garlic:** Heat olive oil in a skillet, add garlic and red pepper flakes, and cook for 1 minute.
3. **Cook shrimp:** Add shrimp and cook for 2-3 minutes per side, until pink. Avoid overcooking.
4. **Deglaze skillet:** Add wine and lemon juice, stir, and season with salt and pepper. Simmer for 2 minutes.
5. **Sterilize jars:** While shrimp cooks, sterilize jars and lids by boiling for 10 minutes.
6. **Fill jars:** Spoon shrimp into jars, leaving 1 inch of headspace. Add cooking liquid to cover shrimp.
7. **Remove air bubbles:** Stir inside the jars to release air bubbles. Adjust headspace if needed.
8. **Seal jars:** Wipe rims, place lids, and tighten bands.
9. **Process in water bath:** Boil jars in a water bath for 10 minutes.
10. **Cool and store:** Cool jars for 12-24 hours. Check seals and store in a cool, dark place.

ADDITIONAL TIPS:

- For a sweeter variation, add a teaspoon (5 ml) of honey to the skillet along with the white wine and lemon juice.
- If you prefer a milder flavor, reduce the amount of red pepper flakes or omit them entirely.

TESTING AND CHECKING THE RECIPE:

- After cooling, check the seals on the jars by pressing down in the center of the lid. If the lid doesn't move, the jar is properly sealed.

STORAGE:

- Store the sealed jars in a cool, dark place. Properly sealed, the canned shrimp should last up to 1 year. Once opened, refrigerate and consume within 2 days.

ANCHOVIES IN GREEN SAUCE

INGREDIENTS:

- 2 lbs (about 0.9 kg) fresh anchovies, cleaned and heads removed
- 1 cup (240 ml) white wine vinegar
- 1/2 cup (120 ml) extra virgin olive oil
- 2 cloves garlic, minced
- 1/2 cup (about 15 g) fresh parsley, finely chopped
- 1 teaspoon (5 ml) salt
- 1/2 teaspoon (2.5 ml) black pepper
- 6 clean pint-sized (about 473 ml) canning jars with lids and bands

INSTRUCTIONS:

1. **Prepare the anchovies:** Rinse and pat dry the cleaned anchovies. Lay them flat in a dish.
2. **Marinate the anchovies:** Combine vinegar, olive oil, garlic, parsley, salt, and pepper. Pour over the anchovies and refrigerate for at least 4 hours or overnight.
3. **Sterilize jars:** Boil the canning jars and lids for 10 minutes to sterilize. Keep them hot until ready to use.
4. **Pack the jars:** Arrange marinated anchovies in the hot jars, leaving 1 inch of headspace. Pour the marinade over the anchovies.
5. **Remove air bubbles:** Stir gently inside the jars to release air bubbles. Adjust headspace as needed.
6. **Seal the jars:** Wipe rims, place lids, and tighten bands.
7. **Process in a water bath:** Boil the jars in a water bath for 10 minutes.
8. **Cool and store:** Cool jars for 12-24 hours. Check seals and store in a cool, dark place.

ADDITIONAL TIPS:

- For a spicier version, add a teaspoon (5 ml) of crushed red pepper flakes to the marinade.
- Ensure the anchovies are fully covered with marinade in the jars to prevent spoilage.

TESTING AND CHECKING THE RECIPE:

- After cooling, check the seals on the jars by pressing down in the center of the lid. If the lid doesn't move, the jar is properly sealed.

STORAGE:

- Store the sealed jars in a cool, dark place. Properly sealed, the canned anchovies in salsa verde should last up to 1 year. Once opened, refrigerate and consume within 2 weeks.

INNOVATIVE AND INTERNATIONAL RECIPES

INTERNATIONAL CHUTNEYS AND SAUCES

MANGO CHILI CHUTNEY

INGREDIENTS:

- ◆ 3 ripe mangoes, peeled and finely chopped (about 1.5 lbs or 680 g)
- ◆ 1 cup (200 g) granulated sugar
- ◆ 1/2 cup (120 ml) apple cider vinegar
- ◆ 1 red chili pepper, finely chopped (remove seeds for less heat)
- ◆ 1 small red onion, finely chopped (about 1/2 cup or 75 g)
- ◆ 1 clove garlic, minced
- ◆ 1/2 teaspoon (2.5 ml) salt
- ◆ 1/4 teaspoon (1.25 ml) ground ginger
- ◆ 1/4 teaspoon (1.25 ml) ground cinnamon
- ◆ 6 clean half-pint (about 240 ml) canning jars with lids and bands

INSTRUCTIONS:

1. **Combine mangoes, sugar, and vinegar:** In a large pot, mix the chopped mangoes, sugar, and vinegar. Stir over medium heat until sugar dissolves.
2. **Add spices:** Add chili, onion, garlic, salt, ginger, and cinnamon. Stir well.
3. **Simmer:** Bring to a boil, reduce heat, and simmer for 45-60 minutes, stirring occasionally until the chutney thickens.
4. **Sterilize jars:** While cooking, sterilize the jars and lids by boiling for 10 minutes.
5. **Fill jars:** Ladle hot chutney into jars, leaving 1/2 inch of headspace.
6. **Remove air bubbles:** Stir gently inside the jars to release air bubbles. Adjust headspace if needed.
7. **Seal jars:** Wipe rims, place lids, and tighten bands.
8. **Water bath process:** Submerge jars in a boiling water bath for 10 minutes.
9. **Cool and store:** Let jars cool for 12-24 hours. Check seals by pressing the lid center. Store in a cool, dark place.

ADDITIONAL TIPS:

- ◆ For a sweeter chutney, you can add more sugar according to your taste. Adjust the amount of chili pepper for desired heat level.
- ◆ For a smoother chutney, blend half the mixture before final cooking.

TESTING AND CHECKING THE RECIPE:

- ◆ To check if the chutney is ready, place a small amount on a cold plate. If it gels and doesn't run when tilted, it's ready to be jarred.

STORAGE:

- ◆ Properly sealed jars last up to 1 year. Once opened, refrigerate and use within 2 months.

INDIAN TOMATO CHUTNEY

INGREDIENTS:

- 4 cups (about 2 lbs or 0.9 kg) ripe tomatoes, chopped
- 1 large onion, finely chopped (about 1 cup or 225 g)
- 1/2 cup (120 ml) white vinegar
- 1/4 cup (50 g) granulated sugar
- 1 tablespoon (15 g) ginger, freshly grated
- 1 tablespoon (15 g) garlic, minced
- 1 teaspoon (5 g) cumin seeds
- 1 teaspoon (5 g) mustard seeds
- 1/2 teaspoon (2.5 g) ground turmeric
- 1/2 teaspoon (2.5 g) chili powder
- 1/4 teaspoon (1.25 g) asafoetida (optional)
- 2 tablespoons (30 ml) vegetable oil and salt to taste
- 6 clean half-pint (about 240 ml) canning jars with lids and bands

INSTRUCTIONS:

1. **Prepare tomatoes and onions:** Chop tomatoes and finely chop the onion.
2. **Cook spices:** Heat oil in a large pot over medium heat. Add mustard and cumin seeds. When they pop, stir in asafoetida (if using), turmeric, and chili powder for 30 seconds.
3. **Add garlic and ginger:** Stir in garlic and ginger, cooking for 1 minute.
4. **Combine with tomatoes and onions:** Add chopped tomatoes and onions to the pot, mixing well.
5. **Add vinegar and sugar:** Stir in vinegar and sugar until dissolved.
6. **Simmer chutney:** Bring to a boil, then reduce heat to low. Simmer for 45-60 minutes, stirring occasionally, until thickened.
7. **Sterilize jars:** While simmering, sterilize jars and lids by boiling them for 10 minutes.
8. **Fill jars:** Ladle chutney into jars, leaving 1/2 inch headspace.
9. **Remove air bubbles:** Stir gently to remove bubbles, adjusting headspace if needed.
10. **Seal jars:** Wipe rims clean, place lids, and screw on bands fingertip tight.
11. **Process in water bath:** Submerge jars in a boiling water bath for 15 minutes.
12. **Cool and store:** Let jars cool for 12-24 hours. Check seals, then store in a cool, dark place.

ADDITIONAL TIPS:

- For a spicier chutney, increase the amount of chili powder according to your taste.
- Asafoetida adds a unique flavor but can be omitted if unavailable.
- Use a non-reactive pot to prevent vinegar reactions.

TESTING AND CHECKING THE RECIPE:

- Test chutney on a cold plate; if it gels and doesn't run, it's ready for jarring.

STORAGE:

- Sealed jars last up to 1 year. Once opened, refrigerate and use within 2 months.

PINEAPPLE GINGER CHUTNEY

INGREDIENTS:

- ◆ 2 cups (about 1 lb or 450g) fresh pineapple, diced
- ◆ 1/4 cup (60ml) apple cider vinegar
- ◆ 1/2 cup (100g) granulated sugar
- ◆ 1 tablespoon (15g) fresh ginger, grated
- ◆ 1 small red onion, finely chopped (about 1/2 cup or 75g)
- ◆ 1 clove garlic, minced
- ◆ 1/4 teaspoon (1.25ml) red pepper flakes (adjust to taste)
- ◆ 1/2 teaspoon (2.5ml) salt
- ◆ 6 clean half-pint (about 240ml) canning jars with lids and bands

INSTRUCTIONS:

1. **Combine pineapple, vinegar, and sugar:** In a large pot, mix diced pineapple, apple cider vinegar, and sugar. Heat over medium until sugar dissolves.
2. **Add ginger, onion, and garlic:** Stir in ginger, onion, garlic, red pepper flakes, and salt. Mix well.
3. **Simmer chutney:** Bring to a boil, then simmer for 30-40 minutes, stirring occasionally, until thickened and pineapple softens.
4. **Prepare jars:** While chutney cooks, sterilize jars and lids by boiling them for 10 minutes.
5. **Fill jars:** Ladle hot chutney into sterilized jars, leaving 1/2 inch (12mm) headspace.
6. **Remove air bubbles:** Stir gently to release air bubbles and adjust headspace if needed.
7. **Seal jars:** Wipe rims clean, place lids on, and screw bands fingertip tight.
8. **Process in water bath:** Submerge jars in a boiling water bath for 10 minutes.
9. **Cool and store:** Cool jars for 12-24 hours. Check seals by pressing lids. Store in a cool, dark place.

ADDITIONAL TIPS:

- ◆ For more sweetness, add extra sugar. Adjust red pepper flakes for more spice.
- ◆ Pineapple can be substituted with mango for a different flavor profile.
- ◆ Always use a non-reactive pot to prevent vinegar reactions.

TESTING AND CHECKING THE RECIPE:

- ◆ To check if the chutney is ready, place a small amount on a cold plate. If it gels and doesn't run when tilted, it's ready to be jarred.

STORAGE:

- ◆ Store the sealed jars in a cool, dark place. Properly sealed, the chutney should last up to 1 year. Once opened, refrigerate and consume within 2 months.

MEXICAN GREEN SAUCE

INGREDIENTS:

- 1 lb (about 450g) tomatillos, husked and rinsed
- 1/2 cup (about 120ml) water
- 2 serrano peppers, stemmed and seeded (adjust to taste for heat)
- 1/2 cup (about 20g) chopped cilantro (coriander leaves)
- 1 medium onion, chopped (about 1 cup or 225g)
- 2 cloves garlic, minced
- 1 tsp (about 5g) salt
- 1/2 tsp (about 2.5g) ground cumin
- 2 tbsp (about 30ml) lime juice
- 6 clean half-pint (about 240ml) canning jars with lids and bands

INSTRUCTIONS:

1. **Cook tomatillos:** Place tomatillos in a saucepan, cover with water, and bring to a boil. Simmer for 10 minutes until soft.
2. **Blend ingredients:** Transfer tomatillos to a blender with water, serrano peppers, cilantro, onion, garlic, salt, and cumin. Blend until smooth.
3. **Simmer salsa:** Return the salsa to the saucepan and simmer for 10 minutes, stirring occasionally.
4. **Add lime juice:** Remove from heat and stir in the lime juice.
5. **Sterilize jars:** While salsa simmers, sterilize jars and lids by boiling them for 10 minutes.
6. **Fill jars:** Ladle hot salsa into sterilized jars, leaving 1/2 inch (12mm) headspace.
7. **Remove air bubbles:** Stir inside the jars to release air bubbles, adjusting headspace as needed.
8. **Seal jars:** Wipe jar rims, place lids, and screw on the bands fingertip tight.
9. **Process in water bath:** Submerge jars in boiling water and process for 15 minutes.
10. **Cool and store:** Let jars cool for 12-24 hours. Check seals and store in a cool, dark place.

ADDITIONAL TIPS:

- For a spicier salsa, keep the seeds in one or both of the serrano peppers.
- You can add a teaspoon of sugar to balance the acidity if desired.
- If the salsa is too thick after blending, you can add a little more water to reach your desired consistency before cooking.

TESTING AND CHECKING THE RECIPE:

- To ensure the salsa has the right consistency, it should coat the back of a spoon and drip slowly when lifted. If it's too runny, simmer for a few more minutes until it thickens.

STORAGE:

- Store the sealed jars in a cool, dark place. Properly sealed, the salsa should last up to 1 year. Once opened, refrigerate and consume within 2 weeks.

ARGENTINIAN CHIMICHURRI SAUCE

INGREDIENTS:

- 1 cup (about 240ml) red wine vinegar
- 3/4 cup (about 180ml) water
- 1 tablespoon (about 15g) salt
- 2 cups (about 480ml) olive oil
- 1 cup (about 240ml) finely chopped fresh parsley
- 1/4 cup (about 60ml) finely chopped fresh oregano
- 6 cloves garlic, minced
- 1 tablespoon (about 15g) red pepper flakes, adjust to taste
- 1 teaspoon (about 5g) ground black pepper
- 6 clean half-pint (about 240ml) canning jars with lids and bands

INSTRUCTIONS:

1. **Combine vinegar, water, and salt:** In a non-reactive saucepan, bring red wine vinegar, water, and salt to a boil, stirring until salt dissolves.
2. **Cool the mixture:** Remove from heat and let it cool to room temperature.
3. **Prepare herbs and garlic:** While cooling, finely chop parsley, oregano, and mince garlic.
4. **Mix the sauce:** In a bowl, combine cooled vinegar mixture with olive oil, parsley, oregano, garlic, red pepper flakes, and black pepper. Stir to combine.
5. **Sterilize jars and lids:** Boil canning jars and lids for at least 10 minutes. Keep warm until ready.
6. **Fill jars:** Ladle chimichurri sauce into jars, leaving 1/2 inch (12mm) headspace.
7. **Remove air bubbles:** Stir inside jars to release air bubbles and adjust headspace if necessary.
8. **Seal jars:** Wipe rims clean, place lids, and screw bands until fingertip tight.
9. **Process in water bath:** Submerge jars in boiling water and process for 15 minutes.
10. **Cool and store:** Let jars cool for 12-24 hours. Check seals and store in a cool, dark place.

ADDITIONAL TIPS:

- For a milder sauce, reduce the amount of red pepper flakes.
- Fresh oregano is preferred for its flavor, but you can substitute with 2 tablespoons of dried oregano if fresh is not available.
- Olive oil can solidify when refrigerated. If using the chimichurri from the fridge, allow it to come to room temperature before serving for the best consistency.

TESTING AND CHECKING THE RECIPE:

- Before sealing the jars, taste the chimichurri to ensure it has the right balance of flavors. Adjust the seasoning if necessary.

STORAGE:

- Store the sealed jars in a cool, dark place. Properly sealed, the chimichurri should last up to 1 year. Once opened, refrigerate and consume within 2 months.

JAPANESE TERIYAKI SAUCE

INGREDIENTS:

- 1/2 cup (120 ml) soy sauce
- 1/2 cup (120 ml) water
- 1/4 cup (50 g) brown sugar
- 2 tablespoons (30 ml) mirin (Japanese sweet rice wine)
- 1 tablespoon (15 ml) rice vinegar
- 1 clove garlic, minced
- 1 teaspoon (5 g) fresh ginger, grated
- 1 tablespoon (15 ml) cornstarch
- 2 tablespoons (30 ml) water (for cornstarch slurry)
- 6 clean half-pint (about 240 ml) canning jars with lids and bands

INSTRUCTIONS:

1. **Mix base ingredients:** In a saucepan, combine soy sauce, water, brown sugar, mirin, and rice vinegar. Stir over medium heat until sugar dissolves.
2. **Add aromatics:** Stir in minced garlic and grated ginger. Bring to a simmer.
3. **Prepare cornstarch slurry:** In a small bowl, mix cornstarch and 2 tbsp of water until smooth.
4. **Thicken sauce:** Slowly whisk the slurry into the sauce and stir constantly until it thickens, about 1-2 minutes.
5. **Cool:** Remove from heat and allow the sauce to cool to room temperature.
6. **Sterilize jars:** While the sauce cools, sterilize the jars and lids by boiling them for 10 minutes.
7. **Fill jars:** Ladle the cooled sauce into jars, leaving 1/2 inch (12mm) headspace.
8. **Remove air bubbles:** Stir inside jars to release air bubbles. Adjust headspace if needed.
9. **Seal jars:** Wipe rims clean, place lids, and screw bands fingertip tight.
10. **Process in water bath:** Submerge jars in boiling water and process for 10 minutes.
11. **Cool and store:** Let the jars cool for 12-24 hours. Check seals and store in a cool, dark place.

ADDITIONAL TIPS:

- For a gluten-free version, use tamari instead of soy sauce.
- Mirin can be substituted with a mix of 1 tablespoon sugar and 1 tablespoon sake if unavailable.
- Adjust the thickness of the sauce to your liking by varying the amount of cornstarch slurry.

TESTING AND CHECKING THE RECIPE:

- To check the consistency of the sauce before jarring, spoon a small amount onto a plate. It should coat the back of a spoon and not run off quickly.

STORAGE:

- Store the sealed jars in a cool, dark place. Properly sealed, the teriyaki sauce should last up to 1 year. Once opened, refrigerate and consume within 2 months

THAI CHILI SAUCE

INGREDIENTS:

- 1 cup (about 240ml) white vinegar
- 1 cup (about 200g) sugar
- 1/2 cup (120ml) water
- 2 tablespoons (30ml) fish sauce
- 10 Thai bird chilies, finely sliced (adjust to taste for heat)
- 3 cloves garlic, minced
- 1 carrot, julienned
- 6 clean half-pint (about 240ml) canning jars with lids and bands

INSTRUCTIONS:

1. **Heat vinegar, sugar, and water:** In a saucepan, combine vinegar, sugar, and water. Heat over medium, stirring until sugar dissolves.
2. **Add fish sauce:** Stir in fish sauce and bring to a simmer. Remove from heat.
3. **Prep chilies, garlic, and carrot:** Slice chilies, mince garlic, and julienne the carrot.
4. **Mix ingredients:** In a bowl, combine chilies, garlic, and carrot. Pour the warm vinegar mixture over the vegetables and stir well.
5. **Sterilize jars:** Boil jars and lids for 10 minutes to sterilize. Keep hot until ready to use.
6. **Fill jars:** Ladle the mixture into jars, distributing the chilies and carrots evenly. Leave 1/2 inch (12 mm) headspace.
7. **Remove air bubbles:** Stir gently inside the jars to release air bubbles. Adjust headspace if needed.
8. **Seal jars:** Wipe rims, place lids, and screw bands fingertip tight.
9. **Process in water bath:** Submerge jars in a boiling water bath for 10 minutes.
10. **Cool and store:** Let jars cool for 12-24 hours. Check seals before storing in a cool, dark place.

ADDITIONAL TIPS:

- For a less spicy salsa, reduce the number of Thai bird chilies.
- The fish sauce adds a depth of flavor but can be omitted for a vegetarian version, adjust the seasoning with salt.
- Wear gloves when handling Thai bird chilies to avoid skin irritation.

TESTING AND CHECKING THE RECIPE:

- Before sealing the jars, taste the salsa to ensure it has the right balance of spicy, sweet, and sour. Adjust the seasoning if necessary.

STORAGE:

- Store the sealed jars in a cool, dark place. Properly sealed, the salsa should last up to 1 year. Once opened, refrigerate and consume within 2 months.

PICO DE GALLO

INGREDIENTS:

- ◆ 04 medium tomatoes, finely chopped (about 2 cups or 480ml)
- ◆ 1 large onion, finely chopped (about 1 cup or 240ml)
- ◆ 2 jalapeño peppers, seeds removed and finely chopped (adjust to taste for heat)
- ◆ 1/2 cup (120ml) cilantro, finely chopped
- ◆ Juice of 2 limes (about 1/4 cup or 60ml)
- ◆ 1 teaspoon (5g) salt, or to taste
- ◆ 1/2 teaspoon (2.5g) black pepper, or to taste
- ◆ 6 clean half-pint (about 240ml) canning jars with lids and bands

INSTRUCTIONS:

1. **Prepare vegetables:** Wash and finely chop tomatoes, onion, jalapeños, and cilantro. Place them in a large bowl.
2. **Mix ingredients:** Add lime juice, salt, and black pepper to the bowl. Stir to combine.
3. **Taste and adjust:** Check seasoning and adjust salt and pepper to your preference.
4. **Sterilize jars:** Boil jars and lids for 10 minutes to sterilize.
5. **Fill jars:** Ladle the salsa into sterilized jars, leaving 1/2 inch (12 mm) headspace.
6. **Remove air bubbles:** Stir gently inside the jars to release any air bubbles, adjusting the headspace as needed.
7. **Seal jars:** Wipe rims, place lids, and screw bands fingertip tight.
8. **Process in water bath:** Submerge jars in boiling water for 15 minutes.
9. **Cool and store:** Let jars cool for 12-24 hours, then check the seals. Store in a cool, dark place.

ADDITIONAL TIPS:

- ◆ For a milder salsa, remove the seeds and membranes from the jalapeños or use fewer peppers.
- ◆ If you prefer a chunkier salsa, chop the vegetables into larger pieces.
- ◆ Lime juice not only adds flavor but also helps preserve the salsa. You can adjust the amount according to your taste.

TESTING AND CHECKING THE RECIPE:

- ◆ Before processing the jars, taste the salsa to ensure it has the right balance of flavors. Adjust the seasoning if necessary.

STORAGE:

- ◆ Store the sealed jars in a cool, dark place. Properly sealed, the salsa should last up to 1 year. Once opened, refrigerate and consume within 2 months.

MANGO LIME SAUCE

- 3 ripe mangoes, peeled and diced (about 3 cups or 720ml)
- Juice of 4 limes (about 1/2 cup or 120ml)
- 1/2 cup (100g) sugar
- 1/4 cup (60ml) water
- 1 tablespoon (15ml) fresh ginger, grated
- 1 small red chili, finely chopped (adjust to taste for heat)
- 1/2 teaspoon (2.5g) salt
- 6 clean half-pint (about 240ml) canning jars with lids and bands

INSTRUCTIONS:

1. **Prepare mangoes:** Peel and dice mangoes into small, even pieces for a consistent texture.
2. **Combine ingredients:** In a medium saucepan, mix mangoes, lime juice, sugar, water, ginger, chili, and salt.
3. **Cook:** Bring to a simmer over medium heat, stirring frequently. Once simmering, reduce heat to low and cook for 20-25 minutes until thickened and mangoes are soft.
4. **Sterilize jars:** While the sauce cooks, sterilize jars and lids by boiling them for 10 minutes. Keep them hot.
5. **Fill jars:** Ladle hot sauce into jars, leaving 1/2 inch (12 mm) of headspace.
6. **Remove air bubbles:** Stir gently inside jars to remove air bubbles, adjusting headspace if needed.
7. **Seal jars:** Wipe rims clean, place lids, and screw on bands until fingertip tight.
8. **Process in water bath:** Submerge jars in boiling water and process for 15 minutes.
9. **Cool and store:** Let jars cool for 12-24 hours. Check seals by pressing down the lids. Store sealed jars in a cool, dark place.

ADDITIONAL TIPS:

- For a milder salsa, remove the seeds from the chili before chopping.
- If you prefer a smoother texture, you can blend half of the mixture before cooking and then combine it with the remaining diced mango for a varied texture.
- Lime juice not only adds flavor but also acts as a natural preservative. Adjust the amount according to your taste and desired acidity.

TESTING AND CHECKING THE RECIPE:

- To test the thickness of the salsa before jarring, spoon a small amount onto a plate and let it cool. It should be thick but not gelatinous, with the mango pieces still discernible.

STORAGE:

- Store the sealed jars in a cool, dark place. Properly sealed, the salsa should last up to 1 year. Once opened, refrigerate and consume within 2 months.

BONUS

I've created something truly special to enhance your canning experience and make your journey into the world of preserving even richer and more enjoyable: **3 exclusive bonuses** filled with valuable extra content that will help you create extraordinary preserves, perfect for every occasion and for a healthy lifestyle.

Just **SCAN THE QR CODES** inside the book for instant access to these extra materials. You can view the bonuses directly on your electronic device or print them out to keep handy in your kitchen.

Delicious Preserves to Gift: An unmissable collection of jams, jellies, and traditional condiments, perfect for creating heartfelt homemade gifts. Each recipe is designed to help you craft preserves that will impress anyone who receives them, making every gift special and unique.

The Ultimate Seasonal Canning Guide: Learn how to make the most of the seasons with our seasonal canning guide. Discover exactly **when** and **how** to preserve fruits and vegetables at their peak, ensuring maximum flavor and freshness all year round.

Canning for Health: Learn how to create delicious, healthy preserves with less sugar and salt—perfect for those on special diets or those looking to lead a healthier lifestyle. These recipes allow you to enjoy genuine, wholesome preserves without compromise.

INGREDIENT INDEX